BioCritiques

Bloom's BioCritiques

THE BRONTË SISTERS

Edited and with an introduction by
Harold Bloom
Sterling Professor of the Humanities
Yale University

CHELSEA HOUSE
PUBLISHERS
An imprint of Infobase Publishing

Bloom's BioCritiques: The Brontë Sisters

Copyright © 2002 by Infobase Publishing
Introduction © 2002 by Harold Bloom

Chelsea House
An imprint of Infobase Publishing
132 West 31st Street
New York NY 10001

ISBN-10: 0-7910-6187-6
ISBN-13: 978-0-7910-6187-9

Library of Congress Cataloging-in-Publication Data
The Brontë Sisters / edited and with an introduction by Harold Bloom.
  p. cm. – (Bloom's biocritiques)
  Includes bibliographical references (p.   ) and index.
  ISBN 0-7910-6187-6
  1. Brontë, Charlotte, 1816–1855. 2. Authors, English—19th century—Biography. 3. Sisters—England—Yorkshire—Biography. 4. Yorkshire (England)—In literature. 5. Women authors, English—Biography. 6. Yorkshire (England)—Biography. 7. Brontë, Emily, 1818–1848. 8. Brontë, Anne, 1820–1849. 9. Brontë family. I. Bloom, Harold. II. Series.
  PR4168 . B756 2002
  823'.809—dc21   2002002187

You can find Chelsea House on the World Wide Web at
http://www.chelseahouse.com

Contributing Editor: Karen Weyant

Printed in the United States of America

IBT EJB 10 9 8 7 6 5 4 3

This book is printed on acid-free paper.

CONTENTS

User's Guide

These volumes are designed to introduce the reader to the life and work of the world's literary masters. Each volume begins with Harold Bloom's essay "The Work in the Writer" and a volume-specific introduction also written by Professor Bloom. Following these unique introductions is an engaging biography that discusses the major life events and important literary accomplishments of the author under consideration.

Furthermore, each volume includes an original critique that not only traces the themes, symbols, and ideas apparent in the author's works, but strives to put those works into cultural and historical perspectives. In addition to the original critique is a brief selection of significant critical essays previously published on the author and his or her works followed by a concise and informative chronology of the writer's life. Finally, each volume concludes with a bibliography of the writer's works, a list of additional readings, and an index of important themes and ideas.

HAROLD BLOOM

The Work in the Writer

Literary biography found its masterpiece in James Boswell's *Life of Samuel Johnson*. Boswell, when he treated Johnson's writings, implicitly commented upon Johnson as found in his work, even as in the great critic's life. Modern instances of literary biography, such as Richard Ellmann's lives of W. B. Yeats, James Joyce, and Oscar Wilde, essentially follow in Boswell's pattern.

That the writer somehow is in the work, we need not doubt, though with William Shakespeare, writer-of-writers, we almost always need to rely upon pure surmise. The exquisite rancidities of the Problem Plays or Dark Comedies seem to express an extraordinary estrangement of Shakespeare from himself. When we read or attend *Troilus and Cressida* and *Measure for Measure*, we may be startled by particular speeches of Ulysses in the first play, or of Vincentio in the second. These speeches, of Ulysses upon hierarchy or upon time, or of Duke Vincentio upon death, are too strong either for their contexts or for the characters of their speakers. The same phenomenon occurs with Parolles, the military impostor of *All's Well That Ends Well*. Utterly disgraced, he nevertheless affirms: "Simply the thing I am/Shall make me live."

In Shakespeare, more even than in his peers, Dante and Cervantes, meaning always starts itself again through excess or overflow. The strongest of Shakespeare's creatures—Falstaff, Hamlet, Iago, Lear, Cleopatra—have an exuberance that is fiercer than their plays can contain. If Ben Jonson was at all correct in his complaint that "Shakespeare wanted art," it could have been only in a sense that he may not have intended. Where do the personalities of Falstaff or Hamlet touch a limit? What was it in Shakespeare that made the two parts of *Henry IV* and *Hamlet* into "plays unlimited"? Neither Falstaff nor Hamlet will be stopped: their wit, their beautiful, laughing speech, their intensity of being—all these are virtually infinite.

In what ways do Falstaff and Hamlet manifest the writer in the work? Evidently, we can never know, or know enough to answer with any authority. But what would happen if we reversed the question, and asked: How did the work form the writer, Shakespeare?

Of Shakespeare's inwardness, his biography tells us nothing. And yet, to an astonishing extent, Shakespeare created our inwardness. At the least, we can speculate that Shakespeare so lived his life as to conceal the depths of his nature, particularly as he rather prematurely aged. We do not have Shakespeare on Shakespeare, as any good reader of the Sonnets comes to realize: they do not constitute a key that unlocks his heart. No sequence of sonnets could be less confessional or more powerfully detached from the poet's self.

The German poet and universal genius, Goethe, affords a superb contrast to Shakespeare. Of Goethe's life, we know more than everything; I wonder sometimes if we know as much about Napoleon or Freud or any other human being who ever has lived, as we know about Goethe. Everywhere, we can find Goethe in his work, so much so that Goethe seems to crowd the writing out, just as Byron and Oscar Wilde seem to usurp their own literary accomplishments. Goethe, cunning beyond measure, nevertheless invested a rival exuberance in his greatest works that could match his personal charisma. The sublime outrageousness of the Second Part of *Faust*, or of the greater lyric and meditative poems, form a Counter-Sublime to Goethe's own daemonic intensity.

Goethe was fascinated by the daemonic in himself; we can doubt that Shakespeare had any such interests. Evidently, Shakespeare abandoned his acting career just before he composed *Measure for Measure* and *Othello*. I surmise that the egregious interventions by Vincentio and Iago displace the actor's energies into a new kind of mischief-making, a fresh opening to a subtler playwriting-within-the-play.

But what had opened Shakespeare to this new awareness? The answer is the work in the writer, *Hamlet* in Shakespeare. One can go further: it was not so much the play, *Hamlet*, as the character Hamlet, who changed Shakespeare's art forever.

Hamlet's personality is so large and varied that it rivals Goethe's own. Ironically Goethe's Faust, his Hamlet, has no personality at all, and is as colorless as Shakespeare himself seems to have chosen to be. Yet nothing could be more colorful than the Second Part of *Faust*, which is peopled by an astonishing array of monsters, grotesque devils, and classical ghosts.

A contrast between Shakespeare and Goethe demonstrates that in each—but in very different ways—we can better find the work in the person, than we can discover that banal entity, the person in the work. Goethe to many of his contemporaries, seemed to be a mortal god. Shakespeare, so far as we know, seemed an affable, rather ordinary fellow, who aged early and became somewhat withdrawn. Yet Faust, though Mephistopheles battles for his soul, is hardly worth the trouble unless you take him as an idea and not as a person. Hamlet is nearly every-idea-in-one, but he is precisely a personality and a person.

Would Hamlet be so astonishingly persuasive if his father's ghost did not haunt him? Falstaff is more alive than Prince Hal, who says that the devil haunts him in the shape of an old fat man. Three years before composing the final *Hamlet*, Shakespeare invented Falstaff, who then never ceased to haunt his creator. Falstaff and Hamlet may be said to best represent the work in the writer, because their influence upon Shakespeare was prodigious. W.H. Auden accurately observed that Falstaff possesses infinite energy: never tired, never bored, and absolutely both witty and happy until Hal's rejection destroys him. Hamlet too has infinite energy, but in him it is more curse than blessing.

Falstaff and Hamlet can be said to occupy the roles in Shakespeare's invented world that Sancho Panza and Don Quixote possess in Cervantes's. Shakespeare's plays from 1610 on (starting with *Twelfth Night*) are thus analogous to the Second Part of Cervantes's epic novel. Sancho and the Don overtly jostle Cervantes for authorship in the Second Part, even as Cervantes battles against the impostor who has pirated a continuation of his work. As a dramatist, Shakespeare manifests the work in the writer more indirectly. Falstaff's prose genius is revived in the scapegoating of Malvolio by Maria and Sir Toby Belch, while Falstaff's darker insights are developed by Feste's melancholic wit. Hamlet's intellectual resourcefulness, already deadly, becomes poisonous in Iago and in Edmund. Yet we have not crossed into the deeper abysses of the work in the writer in later Shakespeare.

No fictive character, before or since, is Falstaff's equal in self-trust. Sir John, whose delight in himself is contagious, has total confidence both in his self-awareness and in the resources of his language. Hamlet, whose self is as strong, and whose language is as copious, nevertheless distrusts both the self and language. Later Shakespeare is, as it were, much under the influence both of Falstaff and of Hamlet, but they tug him in opposite directions. Shakespeare's own copiousness of language is well-nigh incredible: a vocabulary in excess of twenty-one thousand words, almost eighteen hundred of which he coined himself. And of his word-hoard, nearly half are used only once each, as though the perfect setting for each had been found, and need not be repeated. Love for language and faith in language are Falstaffian attributes. Hamlet will darken both that love and that faith in Shakespeare, and perhaps the Sonnets can best be read as Falstaff and Hamlet counterpointing against one another.

Can we surmise how aware Shakespeare was of Falstaff and Hamlet, once they had played themselves into existence? *Henry IV, Part I* appeared in six quarto editions during Shakespeare's lifetime; *Hamlet* possibly had four. Falstaff and Hamlet were played again and again at the Globe, but Shakespeare knew also that they were being read, and he must have had contact with some of those readers. What would it have been like to discuss Falstaff or Hamlet with one of their early readers (presumably also part of their audience at the Globe), if you were the creator of such demiurges? The question would seem nonsensical to most Shakespeare scholars, but then these days they tend to be either ideologues or moldy figs. How can we recover the uncanniness of Falstaff and of Hamlet, when they now have become so familiar?

A writer's influence upon himself is an unexplored problem in criticism, but such an influence is never free from anxieties. The biocritical problem (which this series attempts to explore) can be divided into two areas, difficult to disengage fully. Accomplished works affect the author's life, and also affect her subsequent writings. It is simpler for me to surmise the effect of *Mrs. Dalloway* and *To the Lighthouse* upon Woolf's late *Between the Acts*, than it is to relate Clarissa Dalloway's suicide and Lily Briscoe's capable endurance in art to the tragic death and complex life of Virginia Woolf.

There are writers whose lives were so vivid that they seem sometimes to obscure the literary achievement: Byron, Wilde, Malraux, Hemingway. But most major Western writers do not live that exuberantly, and the greatest of all, Shakespeare, sometimes appears to have adopted the personal mask of colorlessness. And yet there are heroes of literature who struggled titanically with their own eras—Tolstoy, Milton, Victor Hugo—who nevertheless matter more for their works than their lives.

There are great figures—Emily Dickinson, Wallace Stevens, Willa Cather—who seem to have had so little of the full intensity of life when compared to the vitality of their work, that we might almost speak of the work in the work, rather than even of the work in a person. Emily Brontë might well be the extreme instance of such a visionary, surpassing William Blake in that one regard.

I conclude this general introduction to a series of literary bio-critiques by stating a tentative formula or principle for gauging the many ways in which the work influences the person and her subsequent, later work. Our influence upon ourselves is always related to the Shakespearean invention of self-overhearing, which I have written about in several other contexts. Life, as well as poetry and prose, is overheard rather than simply heard. The writer listens to herself as though she were somebody else, and the will to change begins to operate. The forces that live in us include the prior work we have done, and the dreams and waking visions that evade our dismissals.

HAROLD BLOOM

Introduction

1

Can we locate the work in the writer, when the writers are the Brontës? Tuberculosis killed Emily Jane at 30, and Anne at 29. Charlotte died of toxemia of pregnancy, three weeks short of what would have been her 40th birthday. Even Charlotte scarcely had time to be influenced by herself, as it were. In 1847, Charlotte's *Jane Eyre*, Emily's *Wuthering Heights*, and Anne's *Agnes Grey* were published. A year later, Anne brought out *The Tenant of Wildfell Hall*, and Emily died. The next year, 1849, Anne died, and Charlotte published *Shirley*. Two brief years encompassed the Brontë achievement, and their bereavement. In 1853, Charlotte's *Villette* came out, and two years later the last of the Brontë sisters joined the others in death. Charlotte's first novel, *The Professor*, was published posthumously in 1857.

And yet the Brontës, as narrative artists (and as poets), resemble one another far more than they resemble anyone else. Their precursor in a kind of "northern romance" was Sir Walter Scott, but they scarcely have affinities to him. The indubitable forerunner, archetype of Heathcliff and of Rochester, was George Gordon, Lord Byron. The erotic intensity of *Jane Eyre* and *Wuthering Heights* nevertheless seems closer to the novels of Thomas Hardy and D.H. Lawrence, who come after, than to Byron's poems, *Manfred* and *Lara*. The Brontës are self-generated, an autonomous myth in their lives and in their work.

Jane Eyre is a first-person narrative, spoken by its heroine, who is barely distinguishable from Charlotte Brontë. I hardly know another novel in which the narrator is so consistently aggressive toward the reader, who is assumed to be male, more conventional than not, and who needs to be battered into more sensitivity. Since many of us rather enjoy being cudgeled by the Byronic Jane Eyre/Charlotte Brontë, one starts to worry a bit at the sadomasochistic element that invades the book's aesthetic eminence, and seems a vital component thereof. Is not poor Rochester a surrogate for the male reader? Partly crippled, partly blinded, Rochester is tamed into the best of husbands, *totally reliant upon Jane.*

Not only is Rochester a tamed, subdued daemon, but there is daemonic force in the triumphant Jane Eyre, as she tells us of her all-too-happy marriage:

> I have now been married ten years. I know what it is to live entirely for and with what I love best on earth. I hold myself supremely blest—blest beyond what language can express; because I am my husband's life as fully as he is mine. No woman was ever nearer to her mate than I am; ever more absolutely bone of his bone and flesh of his flesh.
>
> I know no weariness of my Edward's society: he knows none of mine, any more than we each do of the pulsation of the heart that beats in our separate bosoms; consequently, we are ever together. To be together is for us to be at once as free as in solitude, as gay as in company. We talk, I believe, all day long: to talk to each other is but a more animated and an audible thinking. All my confidence is bestowed on him, all his confidence is devoted to me; we are precisely suited in character—perfect concord is the result.
>
> Mr. Rochester continued blind the first two years of our union: perhaps it was that circumstance that drew us so very near—that knit us so very close! For I was then his vision, as I am still his right hand. Literally, I was (what he often called me) the apple of his eye. He saw nature—he saw books through me; and never did I weary of gazing for his behalf, and of putting into words the effect of field, tree, town, river, cloud, sunbeam—of the landscape before us; of the weather round us—and impressing by sound on his ear what light could no longer stamp on his eye. Never did I weary of reading to him: never did I

weary of conducting him where he wished to go: of doing for him what he wished to be done. And there was a pleasure in my service, most full, most exquisite, even though sad—because he claimed these services without painful shame or damping humiliation. He loved me so truly that he knew no reluctance in profiting by my attendance: he felt I loved him so fondly that to yield that attendance was to indulge my sweetest wishes.

This startling literalization of Genesis 2:23, Jane's "ever more absolutely bone of his bone and flesh of his flesh," hardly sounds like feminism to my aged (archaic?) ears. Though this famous passage is an idealization, it is saved from the taint of the sentimental by the subtle flavor of the sadomasochistic. At least Lord Byron, dying in the company of the piratical Trelawny and a mercenary troop of Greek brigands, was spared the fate of Edward Rochester, his surrogate.

3

Palpably Byronic, Heathcliff nevertheless is neither a repetition of the Byronic hero (Lara, Manfred, Cain) nor a portrait, however distorted, of Lord Byron himself. Despite his lineage, Heathcliff's greatest distinction as a literary character consists in his originality. As Dorothy Van Ghent strongly emphasized, moral judgment—his own, that of others, or ours—is irrelevant to Heathcliff. A daemonic changeling, Heathcliff emanates from a realm beyond good and evil. His sublimity somehow excludes pathos; his sufferings impress us, but they scarcely move us, so little do they resemble our own. As a representative of what seems before or beyond nature, Heathcliff belongs to the essentially Gnostic cosmos of Emily Brontë's Gondal poems, or of her handful of mature and powerful lyrics. Freedom, for Heathcliff as for his author, resides in the primal Abyss, stationed before the Fall into Creation or our nature. The mutual solitude finally achieved by Heathcliff and the first Catherine, after his death, is at once a wildness and a restoration, and so a freedom very different from that of societal or normative vision.

Melville's Ahab resembles Heathcliff neither in character nor in situation, and yet there is an affinity, possibly because *Moby-Dick*, like *Wuthering Heights*, and like Shakespeare's *Macbeth*, is set in a Gnostic cosmos. Gnostic protagonists manifest a continuous sense of having been outraged; in our time one thinks of Faulkner's Joe Christmas in *Light in August*, or the entire Bundren clan in *As I Lay Dying*. Thomas Pynchon, who appears to be the authentic seer of our contemporary Gnosis, conveys the aesthetics of outrage so persuasively that outrage scarcely seems extreme or uncommon. But there is still a normative and natural world in *Wuthering Heights*; it breaks Catherine Earnshaw, and reduces Heathcliff to the role of the anomaly, who can disrupt for a while, but finally is subsumed by the union of the Earnshaws and Lintons in Hareton and the second Catherine. Yet even as an anomaly, Heathcliff is fiercely memorable, and is as High Romantic as Ahab or as Shelley's Prometheus. All these are questers *contra naturam*, breakers of metaphysical absolutes, who desire what the ruined creation can never give them.

Heathcliff dies by being startled out of life, so distracted by the ghastly presence of Catherine Earnshaw that he can neither eat nor sleep. He is scarcely 38, but has already been essentially posthumous during the 18 years that have passed since his Catherine's death. No one lives for very long in *Wuthering Heights*, or in the Brontë family. My first thought always, when I remember the novel, is that everyone marries very young because they know, on some curious level, that they will die young. Even at his death, the uncanny Heathcliff essentially is an overgrown child, still questing for the union with Catherine he had in his infancy. There are no "mature values" for Emily Brontë, whose imagination, in *Wuthering Heights* and the best poems, identifies transcendent reality with a child's yearnings. Byron's peculiar mixture of sin and guilt, blended from his aristocratic misreadings both of Calvinism and Catholicism, is alien to Emily Brontë, who was not a Christian visionary. Her Gnosticism, very much her own, ignores the stranger God of the ancient heretics, and worships only the God within her own breast. Heathcliff is a follower of that God, whom he calls Catherine Earnshaw.

There are therefore few relevant terms available for describing Heathcliff, since his only quest is for Catherine, alive or dead. But this is not the Shelleyan quest for an epipsyche. Extreme as that was, Shelley remained urbane and ironical enough to acknowledge *some* limits to the name and nature of desire. Heathcliff and Catherine regard themselves as *being* one another, an identification that is neither a metaphor nor a reality. Yet to call it either a delusion or a pathological obsession would be a reduction of Emily Brontë's novel. We are confronted again by the originality of Heathcliff as a fictive character. Frank Kermode wisely remarks of *Wuthering Heights* that: "Dreams, visions, ghosts—the whole pneumatology of the book is only indeterminately related to the natural narrative." There will always be something missing in any critical account of Heathcliff, and of his place in the novel. Emily Brontë, with authentic audacity, declined to provide any bridge except for the fragile though fierce Catherine Earnshaw between the occult and realistic realms in her novel. We lack any certain route into the mystery of Heathcliff.

Aesthetically, this seems to me more of a gain than not, since it saves Heathcliff from psychoanalytic or sociological reductions. His precisely timeless quality is felt in his peculiar relations to present time, where he seems never to be, whether longing for the past, or anticipating a timeless future. The Byronic hero suffers always the crisis of the present, fallen away from the ideal, but Heathcliff has no ideal, not even Catherine, who is too close for idealization. *Wuthering Heights* is of no genre, even as Heathcliff evades the hero-villain category of Shakespeare's Edmund (in *King Lear*) or Byron's Cain. As a protagonist of a kind of daemonic romance, Heathcliff would incarnate some mode of guilt, but even the daemonic is not an adequate descriptive mode for encompassing him. He is so much a negation of every received tradition that he can be seen only as an undoing figure, presumably a blocking agent set against male representations, like Byron's or Shelley's, of the infinite nature of desire. Feminist criticism doubtless will help solve the dilemma of Heathcliff, when some day its instruments of analysis become more refined, but for now, as with all other criticisms, it meets a limit in Emily Brontë's severe modification of the male Romantic tradition. Heathcliff wanders into the nineteenth-century English novel from some unwritten visionary epic, darker and larger than the Gondal saga of Emily Brontë's childhood.

NORMA JEAN LUTZ

Biography of the Brontë Sisters

The Secret Is Revealed

The heavy, noisy Saturday morning traffic on London's Cornhill Street bewildered and amazed the two young women timidly searching for an address. Both were dressed in drab-colored country dresses, lacking in frills or lace. They looked tired, a consequence of their overnight train ride from Keighley to London. They'd had only a few moments to spend in their rented room at the Chapter Coffee House before they had to set out through London's busy streets.

The smaller of the two appeared to be the leader, moving a little ahead of the other. Finally, she stopped and pointed ahead to the bookseller's shop at 65 Cornhill. They had found the address they'd been seeking. As they approached the front entrance, the smaller woman, Charlotte Brontë, once again took the lead as though she were on an important mission. She opened the door, entered, then held it for her sister, Anne Brontë. The shop was filled with young men employed as clerks. They looked askance at the entrance of the two women.

Taking a deep breath, Charlotte approached one of the clerks. "May I see Mr. Smith?" she asked with more boldness than she felt.

The clerk responded with a look of surprise, then told them to wait a moment. He walked toward the back of the store, and Charlotte and Anne sat down. As they looked around the room, they noticed a few familiar-looking books. They had received these same editions as gifts from this very address.

In a small office at the rear of the store, George Smith, the young owner of Smith, Elder & Company, was bent over his desk, anxious to finish his correspondence and go home for the weekend. After his father's death four years earlier, the 25-year-old Smith had taken over his father's publishing business and had rescued it from bankruptcy. That particular morning he was expecting correspondence from his newest author, Currer Bell. Although the author's first novel, *Jane Eyre*, was helping to make Smith, Elder famous, George Smith was currently unhappy with the talented Mr. Bell.

In spite of the fact that the publishing house had gone out of its way to be kind and helpful to Mr. Bell, Smith had recently heard that the author was offering his next novel, *The Tenant of Wildfell Hall*, to a rival publisher. Smith could hardly believe it, especially since Mr. Bell's letters had contained an air of intelligence and integrity.

The tapping on Smith's door at that moment was an unwelcome interruption. The clerk stuck his head in and said, "Two ladies to see you, sir." Smith asked the clerk to find out who they were. In a few moments the clerk returned, saying that the ladies would not give their names and that it was a matter of a private nature. Exasperated and a little short-tempered, Smith told the clerk to inform the ladies that he would be right out. Placing his pen in its holder, he went from his office into the shop. There he saw two "rather quaintly dressed little ladies, pale-faced and anxious-looking," as he later described them.

"Do you wish to see me, Ma'am?" he said to Charlotte.

"Is it Mr. Smith?" she asked, looking up at him through her eyeglasses. The tall young man answered, "It is."

She then placed a letter into his hands—a letter bearing the Smith, Elder return address and addressed to his own author, Currer Bell. He looked at the letter, then looked at the women, puzzled. Charlotte then identified herself as "Miss Brontë," upon which George Smith quickly ushered the sisters into his office. He recognized the name "Brontë" from Currer Bell's address; Bell had requested that he send all correspondence care of a Miss Brontë. Smith had had his suspicions all along that Currer Bell might be a woman. The confusion had been cleared—here in his presence was the real, live Currer Bell. Now the truth about the author's identity could be disclosed at last.

George Smith's office was quite small, with space for only a few chairs and a desk. It was well lit with skylights overhead. When the women were settled in comfortable chairs, Charlotte explained to Mr. Smith that she was Currer Bell, author of *Jane Eyre*. Her sister, Anne, was Acton Bell, author of *Agnes Grey*, a novel released by another publisher, Thomas Cautley Newby. Anne was also the author of the forthcoming *Tenant of Wildfell Hall*. Back at home in the town of Haworth's parsonage was their third sister, Emily, the true author of *Wuthering Heights.* The book, written under the pen name of Ellis Bell, had also been published by Newby. The three sisters had chosen male pseudonyms because in 1848 women's intellectual abilities were considered inferior to those of men.

Rejoicing that there were indeed three separate authors and not caring in the least that they were women, Smith quickly called for his assistant, William Smith Williams. Williams was Charlotte's principal correspondent, and he had sent her copies of the rave reviews of her novel. Williams, a man in his fifties, was more surprised and taken off guard than Smith by the author's gender.

The exuberant Smith was already making plans to introduce the authors to his family and to escort them to parties, museums, and the opera. He could see that this new twist might work as a publicity angle, creating even more sales for the book.

Charlotte quickly doused his enthusiasm. The truth of their identities, she told him, was never to be divulged outside the offices of Smith, Elder & Company. To the world, Currer, Acton, and Ellis Bell must remain as gentlemen authors. Charlotte was firm in her stand that they never be made a public spectacle. The Brontë sisters were too introverted, too shy, too private for such attention—although Charlotte had to admit, inwardly, that she would like to meet some of the more famous authors in London. When George Smith saw he was defeated, he attempted to convince the sisters to stay as guests in his home, where his widowed mother ran the household. Again they refused. Trying one more time, he offered to have his sisters come and meet them that evening. At last Charlotte gave in. She could at least allow him that much.

As soon as the sisters returned to their room, Charlotte's taut nerves and fatigue combined to make her ill. She described her condition as a "thundering headache and harassing sickness." The excitement from travel and the extended interview at the publisher had been too much for a person unaccustomed to cities and strangers. Though she tried to rest, she was not much better when George Smith's sisters arrived later that evening with Smith himself. They were wearing full formal dress, ready to attend the opera.

Charlotte and Anne were not very wealthy and had no such costumes, even in their wardrobes back home at the parsonage. In spite of their embarrassment, they went along. The elegance of the Royal Opera House amazed and enthralled the sisters. Nothing in their secluded, quiet lives could compare with such sights.

Although Smith could not show off his prize author to the public, it did not prevent him from grandly entertaining both ladies. The next morning Mr. Williams arrived in a carriage to accompany them to morning services at St. Stephens, Walbrook. After church they were escorted to Smith's home for dinner. To assuage her feelings of discomfort and embarrassment, Charlotte amused herself with the thought that the guests in Smith's home would have jumped at the chance to meet the author of *Jane Eyre*, and here she sat among them totally unrecognized.

Charlotte and Anne remained in London on Monday, seeing exhibits and dining again with the Smiths. On Tuesday morning, they boarded the train for home, laden with books given to them by Smith, as well as a few gifts they had purchased for Emily and the servants. They had also purchased new gloves and parasols for themselves. The money they spent on their visit to London amounted to more than half of what either of them had once earned in a year as governess. Their success as authors was changing their financial situation. However, literary success, no matter how great, offered the sisters only one small ray of light in the often dark and tragic lives of the entire Brontë family.

TO HAWORTH

It was perfectly fitting that an Irish lad should be born on St. Patrick's Day. Named Patrick, the eldest of 10 children—and the future father of the famous Brontë sisters—was born to Eleanor and Hugh Brunty in 1777 in the parish of Drumballyroney, in County Down, Ireland. Patrick's father was a peasant farmer, and the family lived in a small two-room cottage with a thatched roof. (Because of the illiteracy that prevailed in Ireland at the time, the name went through a series of different spellings: Branty, Brunty, Brunte, Prunty, until Patrick later changed it to Brontë.)

Patrick grew up knowing nothing but poverty. He ate plain fare of buttermilk and bread, with very little meat. The family wore only woolen clothes, the yarn of which was spun, dyed, and carded by Patrick's mother. Although his parents were virtually illiterate, Patrick had a hunger for knowledge. He taught himself to read using the four books he found in their small cottage: his mother's New Testament, his father's Bible, the poems of Robert Burns, and John Bunyan's *Pilgrim's Progress*.

Patrick was first apprenticed as a blacksmith, then as a linen weaver. As he trudged to and from work, he always carried a book in his hands. At age 16, the bright young lad was teaching school, a position he held for five years. In 1798, when Patrick was 21, he was offered a position as tutor for the sons of a widowed Methodist minister, the Reverend Thomas Tighe.

Although Tighe was of the Church of Ireland, he had strong leanings toward the Evangelicals, who were sweeping the British Isles at that time with their message of a personal commitment to God, which began with a conversion experience. John Wesley, one of the more outspoken Evangelicals of the day, was a close friend of Thomas Tighe. Undoubtedly, Patrick's own ideas of faith and religion were strongly influenced by his close relationship with Tighe. It was during this time that Patrick made the choice of his life's work—to be in the ministry. The obstacle that lay in his way was the need for a college education, which he could not afford.

With encouragement from Thomas Tighe, Patrick left his native Ireland and headed for Tighe's alma mater, St. John's College at Cambridge, England. He entered the school as a sizar, one who receives financial aid on the grounds of poverty. In the midst of a crowd of wealthy young English lads, some of whom were 10 years his junior, Patrick threw himself into his studies. His dedication, determination, and hard work would later re-surface in the personalities of his daughters. He made his own way at the school, acquiring no debts and even sending money home to his mother on occasion.

In spite of the fact that he was in competition with the elite of England, Patrick's advancement became something of a legend in the school. He took his degree in 1806 and went on to hold curacies in Weathersfield (Essex), Wellington (Shropshire), and West Riding of Yorkshire.

In 1811, Patrick became a minister at Hartshead. There he met Maria Branwell, a well-educated and highly intelligent woman who caught his fancy. Maria had grown up in the busy port city of Penzance, where the mild climate produced flowers in February. Her family members were among the leaders of the community; they included property owners, investors in the local bank, and members of the town corporation. Maria's brother, Benjamin, served as the town mayor in 1809. The Branwells were also part of Penzance's strong Wesleyan Methodist community, where Wesley himself had often preached.

Upon the death of her father, Maria's uncle Richard (her father's brother) allowed Maria and her two unmarried sisters to remain in the family home. However, after the death of Richard and Richard's son Thomas, the home was sold. Thus Maria moved 400 miles away to be near her aunt and uncle, Jane and John Fennell, who operated a boys' boarding school at Yorkshire.

At the Fennells', Maria became friends with a cousin eight years her junior, named Jane for her mother. Jane was being courted by a young minister named William Morgan, who happened to be a close friend of Patrick Brontë. This relationship gave Patrick a chance to become friendly with Maria much more quickly than would have been normally proper.

Maria, no doubt feeling somewhat misplaced and lonely, was open to the courting of the young Irish minister.

The two couples were married in a double ceremony in December 1812. William officiated at Patrick's wedding, and Patrick at William's. Maria's uncle John Fennell gave her hand in marriage. Patrick was 35, Maria 30.

The couple made their first home in Clough House at Hightown, a mile from the church where Patrick served as minister. These were happy days for Patrick, during which he wrote a book of poems entitled *The Rural Minstrel: A Miscellany of Descriptive Poems*. This was not his first published book. He had previously published *Cottage Poems*, a collection of his writings. Much of Patrick's writing proclaimed the beauty of the natural world, which he saw as the manifestation of a loving God. The influence of his writings would later be seen in the works of daughter Emily and son Branwell.

It was at this home that Patrick and Maria's first two daughters were born. The elder, Maria—named for her mother—was born in 1814, and the younger, Elizabeth—named for Maria's sister—was born in 1815. Shortly after the birth of Elizabeth, Patrick accepted the offer of a position of perpetual curate at Thornton, about 13 miles away. The couple moved into the vicarage, a house somewhat smaller than their previous home, but closer to the church. The Old Bell Chapel, built in 1620, was in a state of disrepair when the Brontës arrived. Patrick did much to fix up the building and breathe new life into its gloomy interior.

In the first few months of life at Thornton, Maria's sister, Elizabeth, came to live with them, perhaps to help with the move. She remained with Maria for the birth of a third daughter, Charlotte (named after another one of Maria's sisters) in 1816. Elizabeth remained with the Brontës for nearly a year before returning to her home in Penzance.

Patrick became a beloved vicar. He worked hard to oversee the villages in the outlying areas of the Bradford district, as well as those located closer to home. Sunday school was particularly important to him, and he encouraged the better educated among his parishioners to teach the classes.

On June 26, 1817, a long-awaited son was born into the Brontë family. He was given two names—Patrick Branwell—one for each side of the family. With four children to care for, the Brontës hired a girl from the nearby Bradford School of Industry—more of an orphanage than a school. Thirteen-year-old Nancy Garrs became a loyal member of the Brontë family, making life much easier for Maria.

In the same year that Branwell was born, Patrick celebrated another event, the publication of his first novella, *The Maid of Killarney*. The book, bearing the imprint of Baldwin, Cradock & Joy, was published anonymously, perhaps because of the love story it contains. This book, of all of Patrick's writings, would have the most influence on his children. According to Juliet Barker, author of *The Brontës*, the passages "describing the beauties of the landscape or singing the praises of the Duke of Wellington could just as easily have been written by one of the Brontë children."

In early spring of 1818, word came that the vicar of the large parish of Haworth, Reverend James Charnock, had died and the position was open. When it was offered to Patrick, he immediately accepted. However, the parishioners at Haworth believed they should be free to choose their own minister. The negative mood among the church members echoed throughout the region, as bad harvests and an industrial depression caused general unrest. Patrick delayed his departure. Meanwhile, another minister stepped in as the vicar at Haworth and received vulgar and unkind treatment. He would eventually leave in defeat.

In the summer of 1818, the Brontës' fourth daughter, Emily Jane, was born and quickly baptized. The child's name was unique in the Brontë family in that none of the Brontës' relations had this name. She was also the only girl in the family given two first names. Perhaps her name reflected her individuality: Emily would become the most unique Brontë, possessed of a singularly sensitive nature.

After the birth of Anne, the last of the Brontës' six children, on January 17, 1820, the house was bursting at the seams. By now, Nancy Garrs's younger sister, Sarah, had arrived to serve as cook while Nancy was promoted to nursemaid. Patrick needed not only higher wages, but a larger house—both of which were promised at Haworth.

Eventually, an appeal was made to the archbishop to settle the problems at Haworth. The license was formally presented to Patrick Brontë in February 1820, naming him the perpetual curate of Haworth. The family's move was delayed for two months, during which time Patrick made the six-mile journey over the moorlands to Haworth whenever needed. This gesture clearly demonstrated his commitment to his new post.

In the latter part of March, baby Anne was baptized in the Old Bell Chapel at Thornton. The next month, the contents of the parsonage on Market Street were loaded onto flatbed wagons, with Maria and the six children settled into the last wagon. The carters yelled at the horses as they strained to draw the heavy wagons up and down the hills between Bradford and Haworth.

The town of Haworth lay on a direct route between Yorkshire and Lancashire, which meant that a constant flow of traffic moved up and down the steep cobbled streets of the town. Situated in the hills above the towns of Keighley and Bradford, its ample water supply made it an ideal site for factories. By the time the Brontë family arrived in 1820, there were some 13 textile mills, most connected with wool. Sandstone quarrying in the surrounding hills created yet another industry. The town itself boasted many businesses, shops, inns, and professionals, including a resident surgeon.

The surrounding moors stretched out in undulating hills of varying colors that changed from season to season. Here, few trees or hedgerows grew, and the trees that survived were bent and twisted beneath the moors' howling winds. These winds blew almost constantly, to the extent that a still day was cause for comment. The wild countryside differed greatly from what the family had been accustomed to.

The wagons carrying the Brontë family and their possessions trundled up the last and steepest hill to where the church and parsonage were located. Built in 1770, the rectangular gray parsonage was made of limestone grit. It faced down into the town, with its back windows overlooking the wide open moors, where the Brontë children would run, play, and find their freedom. At the bottom of the parsonage's garden was the Church of St. Michael and All Angels, where Reverend Brontë would deliver his Sunday sermons for many long years. To the side of the house through a small gate in the wall lay the graveyard, a dreary, jumbled mess of rain-blackened gravestones. It could have been this very graveyard that polluted the drinking water of the Brontë household, bringing on sickness and disease. But had it not been to blame, the lack of proper sewage treatment in the town may have been. The polluted waters of the town contributed to a high mortality rate—the average age of death in Haworth was 25, and 41 percent of babies died before their first birthday. This death rate rivaled the worst districts in London, and it was not a welcome statistic for a family with six young children. For the time being, however, there were no portents of sad days to come.

When the wagons pulled up to the parsonage door, Nancy and Sarah Garrs, been sent ahead to make the place ready, were there to give a cheery welcome. Travel-weary children tumbled out of the wagon and ran inside, anxious to explore the house that must have seemed like a mansion compared with the small cottage they'd left behind.

A WORLD OF THEIR OWN

Patrick Brontë at once immersed himself in the work required by a very large parish. In spite of the problems that had existed before his arrival, he got along well with his parishioners. Having grown up among the working class, he easily identified with them and their problems.

One can't help but wonder about the reaction of the refined Maria to this bleak landscape and the even bleaker house. Having given birth to six children in only seven years, she was in failing health; yet she bravely endured the journey in a jolting, uncomfortable wagon to this new home. Whether she suffered from cancer or blood poisoning from poor postpartum care is not clear, but she was soon confined to her bed.

Maria's illness was difficult for Patrick, who was still a virtual stranger in the community and much too proud to ask for help. Patrick hired a nurse to care for Maria so he could continue with his duties. Later, Patrick sent for Maria's older sister, Elizabeth, to come and help with the ever-increasing workload in the home. In spite of the care she received, Maria died September 15, 1821, less than a year after arriving in Haworth. Before dying she grieved deeply for her six children, crying out continually, "Oh God, my poor children—oh God, my poor children!" At the hour of her death, Maria was surrounded by her family—Patrick and her sister on either side of the bed, and the children at the foot of the bed. Because death was such a common occurrence in those times, children were not shielded from it.

Patrick, sick with grief, was unable to take up his duties for two weeks or more. His greatest concern was, of course, the care and instruction of his children. His sister-in-law would stay only temporarily, since her permanent home was in Penzance. And though Sarah and Nancy Garrs were kind and loyal servants, they were in no position to be instructive. In desperation, Patrick set about finding a new wife.

His first attempt was an old family friend, Elizabeth Firth of Bradford, who was godmother to two of his daughters. His proposal, coming only three months after his wife's death, angered and estranged Miss Firth. It appalled her that Patrick would ask her to take on a penniless clergyman and six little ones. She did not speak to him for two years after his ill-advised proposal. His next attempt was with the sister of the vicar of Keighley, Isabella Dury. She, too, could not imagine taking on the responsibility for six children. Patrick's last effort at seeking a wife and mother for his children was directed at an old acquaintance, still single, whom he had not seen for years. Again, his overtures were clumsy, and he offended the lady rather than attracting her attentions. At that point, he more or less resigned himself to remaining a widower.

Patrick was then successful in persuading Elizabeth Branwell to return to Haworth and help with the children and the running of the household. In spite of the fact that Elizabeth (whom the children called "Aunt Branwell," or simply, "Aunt") hated the cold, windy country and the equally cold, plain house, her sense of duty proved strong enough to overcome her reluctance.

Patrick had a fear of fire, so he never allowed draperies, curtains, rugs, or carpets in his house. This lack of colors and textures tended to intensify the stone house's dreariness and made it seem even more cold and damp. The stone floors were particularly distasteful to Aunt Branwell. She took to wearing wooden pattens—shoes similar to clogs—which kept her feet up off the cold floors. One of the fondest memories often recalled by the Brontë children was the sound of Aunt Branwell's wooden pattens clicking on the stone floors as she moved about the house.

While Aunt Branwell was kind to the children, helping the girls with their sewing work and assisting in running the household, she was not openly affectionate. Because of this, the six children clung closely to one another, with Maria, only seven years old, becoming the mother figure for the group. Maria took over as the nurturing, warm, and thoughtful parent so needed by the younger ones. She had an amazing ability to pour her love and affection in an almost adult manner. The younger children looked up to her and adored her. She was highly intelligent, which caused Patrick to treat her almost like an adult, even at one point trusting her to correct the proofs of one of his long poems.

Because the community of Haworth was made up of uneducated people of the laboring class, Patrick kept his children from associating with the other children of the community. Contacts with the outside world were few; all the children knew was what was contained within the parsonage and what they experienced out on the sweeping, windy moors. Together they took long walks across the moors, talking and laughing, discovering the joys and miracles of nature, and enjoying each other's company. This isolation served to develop the children's bright imaginations. In the upstairs room that came to be known as the "children's study," they spent hours making up plays and acting them out, as well as listening to their older sisters read articles from the most recent London newspapers.

Patrick Brontë's thoughts on the education of girls were a little different from those of most men of his time. Middle class girls were expected to learn basic reading, writing, history, arithmetic, and music in addition to household tasks such as sewing. Intellectually stimulating education, however, was frowned upon, and many leading intellectuals of the day opposed advanced education for women, believing them to be mentally unequipped for such study. In addition, they argued, such education would serve only to distract girls from preparing to be wives and mothers. This opinion was supported by doctors, many of whom claimed that combining the mental demands of education with the physical rigors of menstruation would result in educated mothers bearing a "puny, enfeebled, and sickly race."

Brontë clearly held a different view, as the Cambridge-educated minister served as the personal instructor for his girls and instilled in them his love of literature. All six children devoured the books and periodicals on the shelves of their father's library. They read the *Methodist Magazine*, *Blackwood's Magazine*, the *Times*, *The Arabian Nights*, and John Bunyan's *Pilgrim's Progress*, as well as the writings of Lord Byron, William Wordsworth, Sir Walter Scott, and Robert Southey. Being acquainted with such high-quality reading material gave the children a passion for continual learning.

Artwork also affected and colored their lives. Each of the Brontë children was familiar with the works of Guido Reni, Titian, Raphael, Michelangelo, Leonardo da Vinci, Sir Anthony Vandyke, and others. Hanging on the walls of the parsonage were the apocalyptic engravings of John Martin, which depicted both heavenly and earthly realms—all of which fired the young Brontës' collective imagination.

Although Patrick enjoyed teaching his daughters, he knew he had to plan for their futures. Middle class women had two choices—marry or become governesses—the only paid work available to them throughout most of the nineteenth century. A governess either taught in a school or, more frequently, lived with her employer and oversaw the children not only in lessons, but as a constant companion. In the mid-1800s, there were more than 20,000 governesses in England. They were expected to be moderately educated and genteel, but were always poorly paid.

Realizing that he would never be able to provide his daughters with dowries suitable for them to find wealthy husbands, Patrick began a search for an affordable school. While reading a newspaper one day, he came upon an advertisement for the Clergy Daughters' School at Cowan Bridge. Owned and operated by William Carus Wilson, a wealthy clergyman, the school offered education for the daughters of poor clergymen who could not afford the better schools. The students at Cowan Bridge were trained to be governesses. The school appeared to be the solution Patrick was looking for.

During the spring of 1824, Maria and Elizabeth both suffered from the measles and whooping cough, delaying their enrollment. However, by July, they were deemed fit enough for the 50-mile trip to Cowan Bridge. There, according to the prospectus, the girls were to learn "history, geography, the use of the globes, grammar, writing and arithmetic, all kinds of needlework, and the nicer kinds of household-work, such as getting up fine linen, etc." Mr. Brontë himself accompanied Maria and Elizabeth to the school, and his inspection seemed to have found everything proper and in good order. The elder daughters were tested by the school and found to be lacking in several abilities. This is surprising, because other reports testify to a cleverness and intellect beyond their respective ages; perhaps their extreme shyness prevented them from doing their best on the examinations.

The older girls had been at the school for two weeks when Patrick decided that Charlotte was to join her sisters. Her entry was recorded by school officials on August 10, 1824. Charlotte, too, was assessed as being less able than she was. While she was quiet and withdrawn, perhaps frightened at being away from home, she was still happy to be reunited with her sisters. Mr. Brontë stayed the night and still did not see anything that appeared out of order. He went home to make plans to send Emily to Cowan Bridge in the fall. The school would prove to be a disaster for the Brontës, and it became one of the most bitter experiences of young Charlotte's life.

As an adult, Charlotte would write of the conditions of Cowan Bridge in detailed descriptions in *Jane Eyre*. The school is named Lowood, and the heartless Mr. Brocklehurst was created in the likeness of the Reverend Wilson, the school's founder. Charlotte portrayed the school as being a cold, desolate place with cruel instructors and unbending rules. There was one privy for 60 girls, the food was burned almost beyond recognition, and the dormitory was bare and unheated. The girls were made to walk a long distance to church in the winter cold, then sit for hours in an unheated sanctuary before making the long walk back to the cold dormitory. For the Brontë sisters, accustomed to a warm home, the attention of their nursemaid, the love of father and aunt, and the joys of playing freely across the moors, this amounted to a severe shock.

Charity schools in the Brontës' time were notorious for crowded, unsanitary conditions that by today's standards would be considered extremely abusive. Some of these schools slept six to eight in a bed, with the linens unchanged or unlaundered for months. While Cowan Bridge was not the worst in England at the time, it was bad enough, and years later many attested to the truth of Charlotte's descriptions.

Maria, a dreamy, untidy, and creative child, didn't do well in the structured environment of Cowan Bridge. She constantly took the brunt of ill treatment for her inability to perform. Charlotte watched in horror as her beloved mother figure was taken to task by a particularly cruel teacher, Miss Andrews. When the quiet Maria suffered in silence and did not retaliate, Miss Andrews became even more angry and cruel. Even as Maria grew seriously ill, she was forced to continue with her day-to-day activities. Such treatment incensed Charlotte, and she felt the pain of it for the rest of her life. Eventually, Maria became so ill that Mr. Brontë was called to come and take her home. She died on May 6, 1825, at the age of 11. Elizabeth, Charlotte, and Emily (who had come to the school the previous November) were never able to say good-bye to their sister. For these young children, it was as though they had twice lost their mother. Maria's death may have been even more painful than their mother's; the children were now older and more aware, and they had had years to become accustomed to Maria's gentle love and affection.

As Mr. Brontë suffered through the grief of his second loss, he was unaware that a form of "low typhus" had invaded Cowan Bridge, finding a strong foothold among the malnourished girls. Many of them were already battling colds, fever, and coughing. In May, a doctor was called in to assess the situation. He suggested that the healthiest girls be removed from the infested area. On May 31, Charlotte and Emily traveled with the other children to a seaside house on the Lancashire coast near Morecambe. Elizabeth, too sick to go, was assigned a special chaperone and loaded in a carriage to be taken home. From what existing records show, Mr. Brontë had no knowledge of this removal. As soon as the very ill Elizabeth arrived home, he set out to bring home Charlotte and Emily. Their profound joy at having been taken out of such a nightmarish situation was tempered by the fact that home would be much different without Maria. As tragedy heaped upon tragedy, Elizabeth lived for only two more weeks. On June 15, 1825, she followed her sister to an early grave at the age of 10.

Nine-year-old Charlotte became the eldest sibling, and the worry and responsibility of that position placed a weight on her shoulders that she would carry for years. She acquired a new drive and determination that made it difficult for her to relax or enjoy herself. She stepped into the responsibility of assisting Aunt Branwell with running the household. Charlotte and Emily slowly regained their health with the good food at the parsonage and long walks across the moors in the summer sunshine.

A new face now appeared at the Haworth parsonage, 56-year-old Tabitha Aykroyd, who came to act as the maid. The children gave her the nickname of Tabby, and they loved her dearly. She knew how to discipline them, but she also knew how to have fun, make lively jokes, and tell delightful stories in her Yorkshire dialect. Tabby would live with the family almost continuously until her death at age 84.

The children's education continued, with Mr. Brontë once again serving as instructor. The four were particularly intrigued by geography, and they learned from books such as Thomas Salmon's *New Geographical and Historical Grammar*, Oliver Goldsmith's four-volume *History of England*, Rollin's *History*, and J. Goldsmith's *A Grammar of General Geography*. These books played a large part in the fictional kingdoms that the children would soon create.

Mr. Brontë believed in the importance of reading the Bible. The children had their own copies and knew the contents inside out. Each child also had a prayer book. While Branwell's instruction became more formal and more in-depth than his sisters', it is widely believed that Charlotte,

Emily, and Anne also became well versed in Latin, Greek, and ancient history. The children's favorite magazine was *Blackwood's Magazine*. Its articles, stories, satires, and politics colored their lives and fashioned their thinking. As the four reverted to the games they had played before Cowan Bridge, drama came once again to the forefront. Their plays took on form and substance with definitive titles. Charlotte listed them as *Young Men, Our Fellows,* and the *Islanders.*

The play entitled *Young Men* had its beginnings in a set of wooden soldiers that Mr. Brontë gave Branwell as a gift in 1826. Because Charlotte enjoyed writing down the ordinary details of their lives, she recorded this event. Her father had returned from Leeds late in the night; the next morning Branwell discovered the delightful set of wooden soldiers. Eager to share, he took them to show to his sisters. Charlotte wrote:

> I snatched up one and exclaimed, "This is the Duke of Wellington! This shall be the Duke." When I had said this Emily likewise took one up and said it should be hers; when Anne came down she said one should be hers. Mine was the prettiest of the whole and the tallest, and the most perfect in every part. Emily's was a grave-looking fellow, and we called him "Gravey," Anne's was a queer little thing much like herself, and we called him "Waiting-boy." Branwell chose his and called him "Buonaparte."

Once their heroes were chosen, the children began creating kingdoms in which the toy soldiers would reign. The plays eventually evolved into intricately written stories, maps, and illustrations. Their magazines, as they called them, were tiny, with print so small that most adults could never read them. Keeping the magazines secret added to the fun. Here, they could allow their imaginations to run free, and they were heedless of correct spelling or punctuation. The literature the Brontë children produced at this time would eventually amount to thousands of words.

Branwell decided to base one of these tiny magazines on *Blackwood's* and call it the *Young Men's Magazine*. He planned to be the editor. Charlotte, knowing she was a better writer, later talked him out of it and became the editor herself. Charlotte's stories and articles were not of the domestic things that most 13-year-old girls in the nineteenth century dwelled on. She wrote of war, politics, exploration, feuds, scandals, love affairs, and murder.

Branwell mapped out lands for the magazine, constituting an entire world known as "The Great Glass Town Confederacy." (They later renamed it Verdopolis.) While their stories contained aspects of fantasy, they also contained agencies of the real world: generals, artists, publishers, writers, shops, stores, ships, and miles of highways. The plots became more and more intricate and involved.

The children invented a land called Angria, which at first belonged to all four of them. Eventually, however, Emily and Anne seceded from Angria and created Gondal, a land in the Pacific. For each child, this imaginary world became almost as real, or more real, than events happening around them. Here, they were in charge and they controlled the circumstances. When characters died in Angria and Gondal, they were brought to life again, unlike in the real world.

Reality yanked the children rudely out of their imaginary world in June and July of 1831, when their father became ill with inflammation of the lungs. The illness put him in bed for several weeks. The children were particularly alarmed, since they could not remember their father ever being sick. Although he did recover, he remained physically weak and mentally depressed for quite some time. Patrick realized that if he should die, his children would have nothing; a minister never owned his home. Charlotte, already 14, was just a few years away from being able to earn her own living. However, with only one year of formal education, she had little hope of being hired either as a teacher or governess.

CHARLOTTE LEAVES HOME

The prospects for Branwell's future, in contrast to Charlotte's, had never appeared brighter. He was seen as the most talented member of the family. Although money was scarce, Mr. Brontë procured a painting master for his son. Branwell contemplated being a writer, or perhaps a great poet. As the only son of the family, the world was wide open to him. Not so for his sisters. Patrick Brontë expressed his concerns in a letter to Elizabeth Firth, with whom he was now friendly in spite of her refusal of marriage years earlier. Elizabeth in turn contacted the Atkinsons, a childless couple who had been friends of the Brontës in years past and who were Charlotte's godparents. They proposed to pay Charlotte's tuition to the Roe Head school, an institution that they personally knew to be reputable. There were girls' boarding schools closer to Haworth, but at Roe Head old friends of Patrick's would be nearby to keep an eye out for Charlotte—something he insisted upon after the tragic loss of Maria and Elizabeth.

On a cold, bleak January day in 1831, after Charlotte had handed over the management of Glass Town to Branwell, she climbed into a covered cart for the trip to Roe Head. No doubt her heart was heavy at having to leave home, but her sense of duty was strong. She would have to do well to be of any help to her younger siblings.

Roe Head was quite different from Cowan Bridge. The spacious three-story building was pleasantly located on the gentle slope of Mirfield Moor, overlooking the deep valley of the Calder and the old oak woods of Kirklees. The charming interior featured bow windows, deep window seats, and winding passageways.

Four sisters by the name of Wooler ran the school. Margaret, the eldest, was head of the establishment. A kind and compassionate woman, Margaret was much respected by the 10 or so pupils at the school. A short, stout woman, she wore embroidered white woolen dresses, with her long hair plaited and wound into a coronet upon her head.

When Charlotte arrived at the school, she was observed by a girl named Mary Taylor, who later recorded her impression:

> I first saw her coming out of a covered cart in very old-fashioned clothes, and looking very cold and miserable. She was coming to school at Miss Wooler's. When she appeared in the schoolroom her dress was changed, but just as old. She looked a little old woman, so short-sighted that she always appeared to be seeking something, and moving her head from side to side to catch a sight of it. She was very shy and nervous, and spoke with a strong Irish accent.

Adjusting to the new school proved to be extremely difficult for Charlotte. She knew she was different from the others, not only in her speech, her dress, and her size (she was very small for her age), but also in her looks—she knew full well she was not pretty. In addition, she had poor vision, so she could not see well enough to join in outdoor games. That suited her, however, because she preferred to be alone. Charlotte also had some initial academic difficulties. Having been told by her father that she was of above-average intelligence, she was disturbed to learn that she was lacking in certain subjects, such as grammar. When Miss Wooler told Charlotte that she would have to begin a grade level behind, Charlotte burst into tears.

Only a few days after Charlotte's arrival, another new student came to Roe Head. A year almost to the day younger than Charlotte, Ellen Nussey was a kind, quiet girl, easily befriended the homesick Charlotte. Ellen's first impression of Charlotte was somewhat like Mary's:

> She never seemed to me the unattractive little person others designated her, but certainly she was at this time anything but pretty; even her good points were lost. Her naturally beautiful hair of soft silky brown being then dry and frizzy-looking,

screwed up in tight little curls, showing features that were all the plainer from her exceeding thinness and want of complexion, she looked "dried in." A dark, rusty green stuff dress of old-fashioned make detracted still more from her appearance.

Mary Taylor and Ellen Nussey were poles apart in their respective personalities; however, both became lifelong friends of Charlotte Brontë. Years later, reams of letters written by Charlotte to Ellen would be preserved for the entire world to read and enjoy.

While Charlotte was lacking in several areas of study, it was soon discovered that she had knowledge and wisdom far beyond her years. She amazed them with her knowledge of painting, drawing, politics, Scripture, literary criticism, and poetry. Because she displayed this knowledge without flaunting it, she eventually won the respect of her classmates. Her lack of formal education did not slow her down for long. Charlotte's strong determination and willingness to work hard soon earned her the promotions she longed for.

Education, to Charlotte, was not a luxury, but a responsibility that she took very seriously. Her family was depending on her. While the other girls relaxed, talking before the fire on winter evenings, Charlotte, her nose in a book, would be still studying. She studied so late that the other girls accused her of being able to see in the dark.

Charlotte's storytelling abilities also won the admiration of her fellow students. One night she told a terrifying story of the wanderings of a sleepwalker, which seemed so real and so frightening that one girl who had recently been ill nearly fainted. Charlotte felt so guilty that she resolved never to tell another frightening story again. She did, however, continue to tell tamer stories, which the girls enjoyed immensely.

Because Charlotte was now in close proximity to her father's friends, she was often invited to go visiting. These occasions were times of great distress for Charlotte. Never having been trained in the finer points of manners— which held little interest for her—she was frightened she would commit some grave error that would be an embarrassment to her father. Visiting in the homes of her friends, Ellen and Mary, was more to her liking.

Ellen came from a family with connections and money. The Nussey home was full of the luxuries that the parsonage at Haworth lacked. However, Charlotte thought the family was very boring.

Mary's father—also well-to-do—was in manufacturing, and like Patrick Brontë he encouraged his children to be active in politics. Mary's older brothers were noisy and outspoken and loved to tease. Although Charlotte was almost overwhelmed by their opinions and arguments and could never join in the banter, she learned to enjoy the intellectual stimulation.

Back at Haworth, in Charlotte's absence, Branwell continued to expand Glass Town. He and Charlotte exchanged many letters in which he told her of all the new exploits of their fantasy characters. One day, when Charlotte was particularly homesick, she was told she had a visitor at Roe Head. She went into the parlor to find Branwell, who had walked the 25 miles just to see her. The two spent hours walking in the garden and talking about the latest Glass Town adventures.

During the months Charlotte attended Roe Head, yet another change took place at Haworth. Thrown together as they were, Emily and Anne fused an inseparable friendship. They willingly left Branwell to his own devices and created their own imaginary world together. Charlotte would be the only one of the Brontë girls to form close friendships outside the family circle.

By the end of her third six-month term, in June 1832, Charlotte had achieved far more than the syllabus would normally have allowed. Only once had she received a black mark for failing to learn what had been assigned, and she had won the silver medal for achievement three terms in a row. The school chose to present it to her as a memento of her success. Now it was time for her to return home.

With a strong sense of duty, Charlotte took it as her responsibility to teach her sisters all that she had learned at Roe Head. In a letter to Ellen that same summer, she described her days back at Haworth:

> You ask me to give you a description of the manner in which I have passed every day since I left School: this is soon done, as an account of one day is an account of all. In the morning from nine o'clock to half-past twelve, I instruct my Sisters and draw, then we walk till dinner, after dinner I sew till tea time, and after tea I either read, write, or do a little fancy work or draw, as I please. Thus in one delightful, though somewhat monotonous, course my life is passed. I have only been out to tea twice since I came home.

Realizing the dullness of her friend's existence, Ellen immediately returned with an invitation for Charlotte to come to Rydings for a visit the following fall. Charlotte went, accompanied by her brother, who was in awe of the Nussey home. Ellen noticed the strong relationship between Charlotte and Branwell. It was obvious that Charlotte was exceedingly proud of her gangly, red-haired brother and saw in him signs of great genius and a bright future.

Charlotte's visit was repaid when Ellen came to Haworth the following summer. Just the trip alone was unnerving for the civilized, elegant, and sheltered Miss Nussey. The rough moorlands jolted the open gig in which she was riding, forcing her to walk at times. Ellen was amazed by the old-fashioned way in which the Brontë family lived, as well as by the sparseness of the furnishings in their home. However, she was treated very cordially by Aunt Branwell and Mr. Brontë, and Tabby gushed over her just as she did the Brontë children.

Ellen's descriptions of the house and the people are vivid. Phyllis Bentley, author of *The Brontës and Their World*, summarizes Ellen's impressions. Charlotte's friend noted "the spotless cleanliness, the lack of carpet; the sandstone hall floor and stairs, the walls not papered, but stained 'in a pretty dove-coloured tint'; hair-seated chairs and mahogany tables, bookshelves in Mr. Brontë's study; the clock halfway up the stairs which Mr. Brontë wound up every night on his way to bed, after conducting family prayers and locking the front door."

Ellen saw Aunt Branwell as an old-fashioned lady with huge caps, false curls, pattens on her feet, and a gold snuffbox from which she dipped freely. The girls were all quite small, Ellen noted. Charlotte grew to be only 4 feet 9 inches tall as an adult. Emily was the tallest and the quietest. She was so reserved she could barely make eye contact. Anne was the prettiest of the three and the most personable, in Ellen's opinion.

The sisters and Branwell could hardly wait to take Ellen on a walk to their favorite spots on the moors: the ravines and waterfalls, the caches of wildflowers. Ellen watched as Emily, Anne, and Branwell pulled off boots and stockings and boldly waded into the streams. Timid Charlotte and the proper Ellen waited on the banks until the other three arranged stepping stones so they could cross. Outdoors, Emily lost her reserve and became as carefree and relaxed as a little child. She was, Ellen noted, at one with nature.

In the evenings, Mr. Brontë conducted a family worship service at exactly eight o'clock. Ellen found Mr. Brontë to be an imposing figure with his unruly white hair and the silk cravat that muffled his neck up past his chin, which he wore in hopes of protecting his throat against bronchial attacks. The cravat became his trademark, but it made him look all the more austere. At nine o'clock Mr. Brontë locked and barred the parsonage door and went to bed, leaving the "children" to their own devices. After Ellen's departure, the Brontë household decided they had liked Charlotte's friend as well as or better than any person they'd ever met.

While at Roe Head, Charlotte had stopped writing about her magical and imaginary characters—perhaps her time there had given her the fulfillment she was looking for. Being home again, 17-year-old Charlotte took up her stories, writing more in two years than all the previous years combined. By age 19, Charlotte realized that she might become an old maid. Most girls her age were married and already mothers. There were certainly no eligible men in Haworth. The more she saw her opportunities shrinking, the more she retreated into the land of Angria. As an adult, Charlotte would eventually stop writing about Angria, although she admitted that giving up the fictional kingdom was like saying good-bye to dear friends. Years later, Mrs. Elizabeth Gaskell, Charlotte's biographer, looked at the tiny books she produced and said of them, "The wildest and most incoherent things. They give one the idea of creative power carried to the verge of insanity." All the while, Branwell, never broke away from their imaginary world, as his stories grew more violent and aggressive.

The world of Gondal, created by Anne and Emily, was somewhat different. Although there were passions of high intensity, the morals were the same as the morals of Haworth. In Gondal, evil deeds brought dire consequences, just as they should in real life. The intense melodrama of Gondal was woven into the very essence of Emily's personality and stayed with her all her life. She and Anne would continue to write about Gondal well into adulthood. When Emily was 27 and Anne 25, the two women pretended to be characters of Gondal when they took a trip together to York.

Branwell, meanwhile, entertained passionate dreams of studying at London's Royal Academy of Arts. Mr. Brontë encouraged Branwell at every turn, desiring the best opportunities for his son, although he had no way of paying for them. Then, Providence stepped in. Charlotte received a letter from Miss Wooler at Roe Head, inviting her to take a teaching position; as part of the payment, one sister could attend the school tuition-free. It was the opportunity Charlotte had trained for and yet dreaded, but duty called once again: her labor would pay for Branwell's dreams in London and give Emily the opportunity of a formal education. And, knowing both the school and Miss Woooler gave the position more appeal than that of a governess in a house full of strangers. While Branwell set off with the world at his doorstep, the sisters had to take what little was offered to women of their standing.

VENTURES INTO THE WORLD

Branwell, with his wit, gift for conversation, and aptitude for languages, writing, music, and drawing, could have pursued any one of a number of fields. However, after studying for a time in Haworth under an instructor named William Robinson, an accomplished portraitist, Branwell held an exhibition of his works and became convinced he would be a famous painter. He turned to serious work in oils, producing a study of himself and his sisters in 1835. Later he would paint himself out of the portrait, leaving a faint yellow streak where he had stood. The reason for this is unknown.

While there were closer and other less expensive avenues he could have taken to pursue his study of art, Branwell decided to settle for nothing less than London's Royal Academy. Though Aunt Branwell and Charlotte helped subsidize his venture to London, his attempt turned out to be a miserable failure. In spite of having a pocket full of letters of introduction, Branwell never set foot inside the Academy. He was 18 but had the emotional stability of a child. He'd been indulged and admired yet pushed by his father, who expected great things of his only son. The farther Branwell got from Haworth, the more his confidence dwindled. By the time he arrived in the city, his self-doubt had won. His writings later explained the bewilderment he experienced during the week that he spent in the city. After dropping his things at his lodging place, the Chapter Coffee House in Paternoster Row, he wandered about aimlessly.

> He threaded the dense and bustling crowds and walked for hours, never staying to eat or drink, never calling a coach or attending to personal appearance, but with a wiidish dejected look of poverty-stricken abstraction. His mind was too restless to stop and examine anything.

After seven days of wanderings, he climbed aboard a northbound coach and arrived home with the story that he'd been robbed along the way and had no money to enroll in the school. Now, he was sure his future would be in literature rather than art.

A few months later, Branwell tackled the literary world by submitting works to his favorite magazine, *Blackwood's*. Because his first two submissions were not even acknowledged, his subsequent letters became quite hysterical. With little or diplomacy, he demanded that his pieces be accepted. Somehow Branwell had convinced himself that the aggressive bravado practiced by his fictional characters would win the day for him.

> In letters previous to this I have perhaps spoken too openly respecting the extent of my powers. But I did so because I determined to say what I believed. I know that I am not one of the wretched writers of the day. I know that I possess strength to assist you beyond some of your own contributors; but I wish to make you the judge in this case and give you the benefit of its decision.
>
> Now sir, do not act like a commonplace person, but like a man willing to examine for himself. Do not turn from the naked truth of my letters, but *prove me*—and if I do not stand the proof, I will not farther press myself on you. . . .

Needless to say, Branwell was never published in *Blackwood's Magazine*. Undaunted, he turned his attention to one of the most well-known literary figures in England, William Wordsworth. Branwell sent samples of his work and pleaded for a word of encouragement from the great poet. Again he was met with silence. Branwell again turned his attention to painting. He opened a studio in Bradford, where he planned to become a portrait painter. The merits of his talent are not known, and they would have had little relevance in a town inundated by artists. He returned home once again.

Branwell was not the only Brontë experiencing frustration. Life was as difficult, if not more so, for Charlotte and Emily at Roe Head. Charlotte learned very quickly that there was a vast difference between excelling as a student and trying to teach others to do the same. She never really liked young children and had no patience for foolishness. She described the situation as "stupidity the atmosphere, school-books the employment, assess the society." Longing to have the freedom to write, she went on, "What in all this is there now to remind me of the divine, silent, unseen land of thought, dim now and indefinite as the dream of a dream, the shadow of a shade."

For all of Charlotte's agony, Emily's was worse. She spoke to no one but Charlotte and was unable to eat or sleep. Each day she grew increasingly thinner and paler. Charlotte understood why:

My sister Emily loved the moors. Flowers brighter than the rose bloomed in the blackest of the heath for her—out of a sullen hollow in a livid hill-side, her mind could make an Eden. She found in the bleak solitude many and dear delights; and not the least and best-loved was liberty. Liberty was the breath of Emily's nostrils; without it she perished.

Emily lasted only three short months at Roe Head before she was sent home for her health. Anne came to take her place. She would surprise everyone by remaining at Roe Head for two years, studying diligently and applying herself to the task at hand. This is not to say she was happy there, but she was able to endure.

Charlotte never fully appreciated Anne nor her talents. Both Anne and Charlotte were quite attached to Emily but less so to one another. Thus, each one suffered separately, unable to comfort or console the other. Charlotte had Ellen to turn to in letters, in which she poured her heart out. True to her nature, Ellen quoted Scripture in reply, hoping to assist Charlotte in suffering gladly. In one letter, Charlotte cried out in frustration, "I am not like you. If you knew my thoughts; the dreams that absorb me; and the fiery imaginations that at times eat me up and make me feel Society as it is, wretchedly insipid, you would pity and I daresay despise me."

Charlotte was at this time writing a passion-filled story about the Duke of Zamorna and Mina Laury, remarkable characters who were among some of the best of her "other world" fiction. She felt torn between this writing and accepting the "real world." In the same manner that Branwell wrote to Wordsworth, Charlotte decided to write to Robert Southey, the poet laureate of England. In January while on Christmas holiday from Roe Head, she received her reply from the esteemed poet:

> The daydreams in which you habitually indulge are likely to induce a distempered state of mind. . . . Literature cannot be the business of a woman's life, and it ought not to be. The more she is engaged on her proper duties, the less leisure will she have for it, even as an accomplishment and a recreation.

Charlotte received the reprimand from the male literary establishment quietly. She replied to his letter, thanking him for his wise advice and promising never to forget it. Privately, she resolved to quit her "world below" and wrote a long and tragic farewell to it.

In 1837, because of the illness of Miss Wooler's father, Roe Head School was moved to Dewsbury Moor. Charlotte did not like the new location, nor did she appreciate the fact that Miss Wooler had to be gone for long periods of time. Another Wooler sister, Eliza, arrived to take command. Almost at once, Anne's health began to fail, which greatly alarmed Charlotte. Vivid memories of the deaths of her two older sisters possibly caused her to overreact. She accused Eliza Wooler previously of being callous to Anne's needs. This resulted in a sharp confrontation between Charlotte and Margaret Wooler, who had become a fairly close friend. The friendship was later mended, mostly on Miss Wooler's initiative. In the meantime, in December 1837, Anne left Dewsbury Moor after two full years of study. Charlotte was alone again.

To everyone's surprise, Emily ventured out on her own, accepting a post as governess in a girl's boarding school known as Law Hill, at Southowram outside of Halifax. Her workload there was unbelievable. Charlotte described Emily's post in a letter to Ellen as being from six in the morning until eleven at night. She called it "slavery." It is not known for sure how long Emily lasted at Law Hill. However, in spite of the long hours, she continued to write poems—some of Gondal, some of Yorkshire. Law Hill is close to High Sunderland and Shibden Hall, both of which factor in Emily's novel, *Wuthering Heights*.

In the spring of 1838, Charlotte finally gave up teaching at Roe Head and returned to Haworth. She left under doctor's orders that she must return home if she valued her life. By this time, her spirits were at their lowest ebb. It did not take her long to recover as she enjoyed the peace, quiet, and familiarity of home. For a number of months, all four Brontë children were once again at home.

In the spring of 1839, Charlotte received a letter from Reverend Henry Nussey, Ellen's elder brother, containing a formal proposal of marriage. Most women in Charlotte's position would have jumped at this opportunity. Not only was Henry a respected vicar, but if Charlotte married him, Ellen would become her true sister. However, she did not have strong feelings for him, so she kindly refused him. They remained friends.

The next month, Anne set out to become a governess in the family of Mrs. Ingham at Blake Hall, Mirfield. More suited to being a governess than either of her older sisters, Anne was more settled in her ways, had a milder personality, and cared for children more than Emily or Charlotte. Within a few weeks of Anne's departure, Charlotte left to take a post as governess in Mrs. Sidgwick's family at Stonegappe near Skipton. This became a disaster, for the children were deplorable. ". . . more riotous, perverse, unmanageable cubs never grew," she wrote to Ellen. In addition, so much extra sewing work was heaped on her that she had no time to herself. She left in July.

That same summer, Charlotte received yet another proposal of marriage. This one was from a young curate, the Reverend James Bryce. He had recently come to Haworth with his vicar to pay his respects to Mr. Brontë. He was delighted by Charlotte, making her laugh with his Irish jokes. Only a few days after his departure, she received his proposal by mail, but promptly refused.

For months, Ellen had been encouraging Charlotte to come for a long visit, but matters at Haworth contributed to a long delay. In September, they were finally able to take a holiday together at the seaside at Bridlington. Spending a quiet week there, Charlotte found she had a deep passion for the sea. She returned home much refreshed.

Unfortunately, Tabby became ill near the end of 1839 and had to leave her long-standing post of loving cook and housekeeper for the Brontës. They looked forward to her possible return and refused to bring a stranger into the house temporarily. Charlotte, in a letter to Ellen, explained that Emily did the baking, while Charlotte kept the rooms clean and attempted to learn how to iron. "I excited Aunt's wrath very much by burning the cloth[e]s the first time I attempted to iron but I do better now."

A bright light entered the lives of the Brontë family when a young curate came to work alongside Mr. Brontë. William Weightman, called

Willie by the family (or teasingly referred to as Celia-Amelia because of his pretty appearance), was a handsome and personable fellow with a degree from Durham University. Well read but not dull or stuffy, he added a new dimension to the lives of the four Brontë children. Branwell idolized Willie, and the girls fussed over him.

Charlotte was the first to carefully guard her heart, for she could see that the good-looking Willie flirted with every girl he met. Anne, on the other hand, was not so fortunate. Her future writings indicate that she fell deeply in love with the new curate. However, it was not her destiny to be his wife. In August 1840, Anne once again left home to serve as a governess, this time for the family of Mr. Robinson, a country landowner at Thorp Green in York.

During these years, Branwell became active in community affairs, playing the church organ, teaching Sunday school, and serving as secretary for the local temperance society. His friendship with the church sexton, John Brown, may have helped to turn him astray. Branwell began spending much time with Brown, and Brown spent much time at the tavern in the Black Bull Hotel in Haworth.

A month after Anne left for Thorp Green, Branwell took a job as a clerk at the railway station. The railroad at that time represented the future, and a job at the station was respectable. All went well for a time, but eventually Branwell fell in with a band of mill owners, with whom he drank and quarreled. In March 1842, he was dismissed for increasing carelessness in his books, which were a combination of railway notations and Angrian and Yorkshire poems and drawings. Again, Branwell came home in disgrace.

Charlotte bravely attempted another position as governess, this time with the White family of Upperwood House in Leeds. This position was an improvement over her previous one in that the children were better behaved and the parents more civil. Charlotte did a lot of thinking, assessing, and planning while at Leeds. She pondered the means by which none would need to serve as governesses. She began to think of opening their own school.

What would happen, she wondered, if the Brontë sisters started a school of their own!

Traveling Abroad

As Charlotte warmed up to her new plan, she shared the idea with her sisters and her friends. She even felt comfortable enough to share her idea with her employers, the Whites, who added their encouragement. By chance, Miss Wooler wrote to Charlotte to offer her the Woolers' school. This option was also given serious consideration. However, a piece of the puzzle was still missing—of the three sisters, none was well versed enough in foreign languages to be able to run a school. They would all need further education. With this in mind, Charlotte wrote a serious, businesslike letter to Aunt Branwell, asking her to fund a trip to the continent for her and Emily so they could study French, German, and perhaps Italian as well. Aunt Branwell surprised Charlotte by agreeing wholeheartedly to the plan.

Even though Emily had previously proved that she could not exist away from her beloved moors, Charlotte seemed to want to give her another chance. Anne, at the time, was gainfully employed and had already received two years of formal education, making her the clear choice. And Charlotte may have had an ulterior motive for traveling abroad. Mary Taylor, Charlotte's childhood friend, had recently traveled in Belgium and Holland with her brother Joe. Her letters to Charlotte described beautiful places, the likes of which Charlotte had never seen. Suddenly her world seemed very small, and she was more than ready to break out.

In a flurry of letter writing, Charlotte discovered a school in Brussels that they could possibly afford, the Pensionnat Héger. As soon as she read the information outlining what the school had to offer, she wrote to Madame Héger, the school's owner. The simple and urgent tone of Charlotte's letter appealed to Madame Héger, and Charlotte and Emily were accepted.

While Charlotte fussed over details and decided which direction to take in the quest to set up a school, quiet Emily became willing, but not enthusiastic. In a diary that she and Anne had agreed to write every four years, she revealed her feelings in the matter:

> A scheme is at present in agitation for setting us up in a school of
> our own; as yet nothing is determined, but I hope and trust it
> may go on and prosper and answer our highest expectations.

It would appear that Emily did not want to fail her family this time and was determined to make this work, no matter what it required of her.

Mr. Brontë at first was not overly in favor of the plan, but he later softened and even agreed to accompany his daughters on their journey to Brussels. The first leg of their journey would be a stop in London, where Mr. Brontë secured lodgings at the Chapter Coffee House, the only hostelry he knew in the city (the same place where Branwell had lolled away his week in London several years earlier). They had all agreed to spend three days sightseeing in London. Mary and Joe Taylor kindly offered to come to London and serve as their guides. Mary would later remember Charlotte's eagerness to see all she could in a short amount of time. "She seemed to think our business was and ought to be, to see all the pictures and statues we could. She knew the artists and knew where other productions of theirs were to be found."

On February 12, 1842, Mr. Brontë, Charlotte, and Emily set sail for Belgium on a packet, a ship carrying passengers, mail, and cargo. They left from a wharf near London Bridge for the 14-hour voyage across the English Channel. The travelers then took a coach to Brussels, where they entered a whole new world. Mr. Brontë deposited his daughters safely behind the high walls of the Pensionnat, then left to return home.

The Pensionnat was beautifully arranged in a large quadrangle of buildings, playgrounds, and large lush gardens. For any city dweller, there was more than enough "outdoors." However, for a person accustomed to miles and miles of open space, as Emily and Charlotte were, it would have seemed much more confining.

Despite their initial enthusiasm, the sisters suffered from loneliness. Not only were Charlotte and Emily "foreigners" among the Belgian and French girls, they were also the only Protestants among Catholics. At ages 24 and 26, they were the oldest students there, and they were dressed in clothes that must have seemed terribly old-fashioned and out of style. Madam Héger, sensing their need for privacy, arranged for the Brontë sisters to lodge in a curtained-off area at the end of the long dormitory. This at least kept them apart from the stares and whispers of the others. Charlotte and Emily did little to bridge the gap with their peers. They made no efforts to make friends and instead clung to one another. Their shyness, together with their deep distrust for anything that smacked of Catholicism, kept the walls of isolation firm.

The school was culturally different from girls' schools in England. For one, it was not run by spinsters. Madame Héger was very much married and in fact gave birth to a son not long after the sisters' arrival. Furthermore, she already had three daughters who had the run of the school grounds. Her husband, Constantin Héger, a visiting professor, taught French and mathematics at a boys' school and literature at his wife's school. The subjects offered at the Pensionnat included French, drawing, music, singing, writing, arithmetic, and German. In spite of the fact that Charlotte had moved from the position of teacher back to that of student, she was happy in her studies. She admitted in a letter to Ellen that she was so busy the time fairly flew by.

Monsieur Héger was at first a puzzlement to Charlotte. His teaching abilities were known throughout Brussels, and he offered to give both Charlotte and Emily private attention to help them in their French diction. Charlotte described him to Ellen as "a professor of rhetoric, a man of power as to mind, but very choleric and irritable as to temperament; a little black ugly being, with a face that varies in expression. Sometimes he borrows the lineaments of an insane tom-cat, sometime those of a delirious hyena. . . ."

When the professor became angry with Charlotte, she would cry. Emily never wilted before him. She needed no male affirmation to define her identity. Emily bewildered the professor, who, noting her brilliant mind, later lamented that she had not been born a man.

In September, Madame Héger proposed that Charlotte and Emily remain another half year, and she offered to hire Charlotte as a part-time English instructor and Emily as a part-time music teacher. This would allow them to continue their studies in French and German. The sisters were tempted to accept; however, several distressing events precluded their staying on. It was at this time that the delightful, constantly happy Willie Weightman fell ill with cholera and died on September 6, with Branwell by his side. Weightman had probably been the only close friend Branwell had ever had, and now he was gone. In Brussels, the news shocked and disturbed Charlotte and Emily. They had laughed and flirted with Willie and teased him, and they loved him like a brother. Anne may have loved him even more deeply. But of all the Brontë children, only Branwell was on hand to attend the funeral.

Close on the heels of this tragedy came the news that Mary Taylor's younger sister, Martha, had also died of cholera. The Taylor sisters were in Brussels at the time of Martha's death. Mary, Martha, Charlotte, and Emily had spent many happy hours together.

At the Haworth parsonage, a third tragedy was unfolding. Aunt Branwell had fallen seriously ill. Only two days after Martha's funeral, Charlotte and Emily received the letter informing them of their aunt's illness. They hurriedly pursued plans to pack and leave for home. But before they could even leave the city, a letter came bearing the news of their beloved's aunt's death.

These losses were particularly difficult for Branwell, who was left to suffer alone while tending to the two whom he loved so dearly. In a letter to a friend, he apologized and explained why he had not written.

> There is no misunderstanding. I have had a long attendance at the death-bed of the Rev. Mr. Weightman, one of my dearest friends, and now I am attending at the death-bed of my aunt, who has been for twenty years as my mother. I expect her to die in a few hours. . . .

The girls returned to an even more bare and gloomy house. The sounds of their aunt's wooden pattens clicking about the house would now silenced.

All the love and attention she had given them, at the sacrifice of her own comfort and pleasures, would not be forgotten.

Emily was glad to be home. By contrast, Charlotte struggled with a strange restlessness. With Anne still employed at Thorp Green and Aunt Branwell gone, it feall to Emily to manage the household. She took on the job with great pleasure.

Fortunately, their aunt left each of the girls a comfortable sum of money as their inheritance. She left none to Branwell, however, as she must have imagined he would be well into a successful career by the time of her death. Nothing could be further from the truth. His latest disaster with the railway company could not be attributed to childish irresponsibility or youthful indiscretion. He was a grown man who had been unable to hold down the simplest of jobs—that of a railway clerk. His feelings of failure were beginning to consume him. Soft-hearted Anne no doubt felt sorry for her brother. When she learned that her employers, the Robinsons, were looking to hire a tutor for their young son, she suggested they hire Branwell.

With everyone thus well positioned, Charlotte could return to Brussels with a clear conscience. She had arrived home carrying a letter from the Hégers addressed to Mr. Brontë, which extolled Charlotte's virtues and requested that he allow her to return as a teacher. At age 65, and with his eyesight failing, Mr. Brontë must have struggled with the difficult decision to allow his eldest daughter to leave once again. Eventually, he did give his consent. In a decision she would later regret, Charlotte left for Brussels alone in January 1843.

TROUBLED TIMES

To become a teacher among the girls at the Pensionnat—girls even more spoiled than their English counterparts—was a daunting task, especially for a foreigner and a woman the size of a child. However, the determined Charlotte soon commanded their respect and proved an excellent English instructor.

Weeks passed before Charlotte realized that she had a deep-seated, almost unconscious reason for returning to the school—she was in love with Constantin Héger. Although she could not admit this to herself for a time, Mme. Héger, a woman quite worldly-wise, could see it plainly. With the shrewdness of a smart wife and a business owner who wanted no hint of scandal in her school, Mme. Héger began to engineer the separation of her husband from the young English girl. Whereas Charlotte had previously been allowed to teach English to M. Héger and his brother-in-law, the two men suddenly became too busy for the lessons to continue. Charlotte no longer found the professor in places where she would previously "happen" to run into him. While he still gave her gifts of inscribed books, he ceased to engage in any lengthy conversations with her. In addition, Mme. Héger, who was once friendly and warm, became cool and aloof. The joy Charlotte felt upon her return to Brussels soon grew into dejection and intense loneliness. After all, the Hégers had been her only friends at the school; without their company she was lost and alone.

By the time the summer holidays arrived and the school had emptied, Charlotte was even more morose. Letters from Mary Taylor in Germany begged Charlotte to join her there. She was tutoring young German boys and insisted that there was plenty of work for two. Charlotte refused. Ellen begged her to come home to England. Again Charlotte refused. She was being held by emotions that were new and strange to her. She'd never been in love before.

It was Mme. Héger's plan for Charlotte to become so miserable that she would eventually resign and go home. The plan very nearly worked. In October, Charlotte could bear no more. Hurrying into Madame's sitting room one day, she asked to take her leave. The resignation was accepted on the spot. However, neither woman had reckoned with M. Héger. When he learned the news, he protested vehemently, insisting almost in anger that Charlotte stay. His anger, in Charlotte's mind, proved that he did care about her in spite of what his wife said or did. She agreed to stay, but nothing changed. Charlotte's misery increased until she at last chose to leave in January 1844. When the students at the school realized Charlotte was going away for good, they poured out their sentiments to her. This was a great surprise; Charlotte had no idea they cared about her at all. But then she'd never opened the door of her heart to allow them to display their affection.

Charlotte's obsession with the professor became more exaggerated after her return to England. She could think of nothing but Constantin Héger. She wrote to him, somewhat guardedly, yet revealing her sense of longing. When no reply came, she was in agony. For months, she eagerly awaited each day for a letter from him: "Day and night I find neither rest nor peace. . . . If my master withdraws his friendship from me entirely, I shall be altogether without hope," she wrote. Later the despair is even more evident as she writes, "To forbid me to write to you, to refuse to answer me, would be to tear from me my only joy on earth. . . . When day by day I await a letter, and when day by day disappointment comes . . . I lose appetite and sleep—I pine away."

Professor Héger tore up Charlotte's letters and threw them away. However, Mme. Héger was not so ready to dispose of them. Perhaps she felt she might one day need them for evidence. She rescued them from the wastebasket, carefully stitched the pieces back together, and tucked them away. (The discreet family did not produce the letters to the public until several years after the death of Charlotte's husband, Arthur Nicholls, whom she married in 1854.) Charlotte would later use M. Héger as the pattern for the character of Mr. Rochester in her famous novel, *Jane Eyre*. Years later, when Mrs. Gaskell, Charlotte's biographer, came across these letters, she must have been disturbed. She included in the biography careful extracts from only two letters, and the picture of M. Héger she used was one of him as an elderly man. Because her book came out so soon after Charlotte's death, the biographer obviously felt a great responsibility for preserving Charlotte's good reputation.

Throughout this time of pining, to Charlotte's credit, she attempted to move forward with the plan for a school governed by the Brontë sisters. At first, they sought locations in areas other than Haworth. Their father's failing eyesight squelched that plan, for he could not be left alone. It became more evident that if there were to be a school, it would have to be at the parsonage. If the school proved to be successful, another wing could be added to the house.

The sisters designed flyers and had them printed. Charlotte wrote to friends and acquaintances who might have daughters of school age, but no pupils were forthcoming. Possibly it was the thought of the barren countryside and the gloomy house that kept prospects away. In a letter to Ellen, who also helped to distribute flyers, Charlotte admitted defeat: " . . . depend upon it, Ellen, if you were to persuade a mamma to bring her child to Haworth—the aspect of the place would frighten her and she would probably take the dear thing back with her instanter."

Charlotte celebrated her 30th birthday full of discouragement, feeling as if she had accomplished nothing with her life. The previous March, Charlotte had received word that her good friend Mary Taylor had sailed for New Zealand, determined to make it on her own in another country. Charlotte couldn't help but envy her friend's freedom. Because of her father's failing eyesight, she could not leave him. Charlotte had to carry out any business of the parsonage that required traveling into town, because Emily never traveled.

The family was surprised when Anne returned home from Thorp Green in the summer of 1845. Her reason for leaving, she said, was because the children were past governessing age. But Branwell had also quit Thorp Green, offering no excuses at all. Charlotte gave no thought to their reasons—she was too happy to see them to ask questions. With Anne at home, she was now free to be released from the prison of Haworth to visit Ellen.

When her refreshing two weeks with Ellen were over, Charlotte had a premonition that she would be returning home to some new sorrow. Upon her return, she learned the truth of Branwell's departure from Thorp Green: He had been accused by Mr. Robinson of having a love affair with Robinson's wife. In light of the embarrassment, Anne saw no recourse but to leave as well. Charlotte was devastated. She too had fallen in love with someone who was married, but she had suffered in silence and no one but the Hégers knew. Branwell, on the other hand, raved in anguish, attempting to draw pity from others in the household. According to him, he'd been seduced by the older woman and was totally innocent. Mr. Brontë agreed, calling Mrs. Robinson a "diabolical seducer." Even Anne felt sorry for Branwell in spite of the fact that she'd lost her position over his misbehavior. Whether or not Branwell truly loved Mrs. Robinson may never be known, but he held out hope that she would leave her husband and marry him. In his mind, he was saving her from a cruel spouse. In a letter to a friend, Branwell admitted that Mr. Robinson had threatened to shoot him if he ever returned to Thorp Green.

From this time forward, Branwell spent more and more time with his drinking companions. Often coming home drunk, his behavior ranged from intense rage to dejected self-pity. Eventually, the gin gave way to opium, which he purchased by borrowing money from whomever he could.

Charlotte was the most social member of the family, but she felt she could invite no one to the parsonage during this time. She wrote to Ellen insisting that she not come visit while Branwell was displaying such erratic behavior. Even if the Brontës had been able to start a school, Branwell's behavior would have made keeping students at the parsonage impossible.

All the plans of all four Brontë children seemed to have met with failure. It was clear that Branwell would never shoulder any financial or other responsibility for the family. While Anne and Emily, along with Mr. Brontë, continued to care for and support Branwell as best they could, Charlotte had had her fill of him. She poured out her agony in a letter to Ellen in 1845.

> I can hardly tell you how time gets on at Haworth. There is no event whatever to mark its progress—one day resembles another. . . . There was a time when Haworth was a very pleasant place to me, it is not so now. I feel as if we were all buried here—I long to travel, to work, to live a life of action.

While Charlotte and Branwell were in anguish, Emily and Anne reverted back to their twin-like friendship, talking and writing together and taking long walks out across the moors. It took very little for Emily to be contented. In her diary from the summer of 1845, she mentions that she and

Anne still wrote about the Gondals. She also explained about the failure of the school, adding, "Now I don't desire a school at all, and none of us have any great longing for it." Her attitude toward the problems with Branwell are then expressed in her own undisturbed manner: "We are all in decent health, only that papa has a complaint in his eyes, and with the exception of B., who, I hope, will be better and do better hereafter. I am quite contented for myself. . . ."

In the ensuing months, Branwell did make attempts to find employment, but sensing Charlotte's anger and disappointment toward him, he did not share this with her. When his attempts failed, he buried his sorrow in further drinking.

At the moment when life appeared its bleakest, Charlotte chanced upon a volume of verse written by Emily. She was first surprised, then deeply impressed by the quality of her sister's writing: "The pieces are short, but they are very genuine; they stirred my heart like the sound of a trumpet when I read them alone and in secret."

From childhood, all the Brontës harbored dreams of being published authors. Charlotte now began to see that their dreams might come true. But convincing the reclusive Emily of this fact would not be easy. Indeed, Emily was insulted that Charlotte had read her work in the first place, and she would not hear of it being published. Anne then admitted that she, too, had poetry that she could add to a published volume. This quieted Emily somewhat.

Behind closed doors, the three sisters formulated their plans. All three would contribute to a book of verse, and Charlotte would write letters to find a publisher. But first they made the firm decision to keep their identities secret. They further decided that their pseudonyms would be male. Male poets, after all, would be accepted with much more credibility than female ones.

Keeping their initials the same, they chose Currer, Ellis, and Acton Bell. The last name of Bell was taken from the new curate who had come to help Mr. Brontë, Arthur Bell Nicholls.

As they were busily working to edit their works and choosing which selections to submit, another crisis hit Branwell's life. Word came that Mr. Robinson had died. Branwell assumed he would now be called for by his lover, Mrs. Robinson. Not only would he have her love, but her money as well. And word did come, but it was not what Branwell expected. He was told that Mr. Robinson stated in his will that if his wife ever spoke to Branwell Brontë again, she must forfeit her right to any money she inherited. Branwell was crushed. He would have been even more crushed had he known it was all a lie. Mrs. Robinson was free to marry whomever she pleased, but she had long ago tired of the young man.

Branwell's behavior became so reckless that he endangered his family. One night he fell into bed in a drunken stupor with a candle burning and very nearly set the house on fire. Only Emily's quick thinking and quick action saved them from tragedy. From then on, Mr. Brontë insisted that his wayward son sleep in his bedroom.

After a long search, Aylott and Jones Publishers in London agreed to publish the sisters' poems, but at the authors' expense. So, they used a portion of their inheritance money from Aunt Branwell. . The publication run on the book was 1,000 copies, of which only two were sold. On the surface, the venture appeared to be a failure. On the brighter side, the reviews were good and gave the sisters courage for future ventures. If they could be published once, surely it could happen again. One reviewer wrote: "It is a long time since we have enjoyed a volume of such genuine poetry as this. . . . This small book of some 170 pages only has come like a ray of sunshine, gladdening the eye with present glory and the heart with promise of bright hours in store."

Charlotte wrote to Aylott and Jones, revealing that they were not giving up:

C. E. & A. Bell are now preparing for the Press a work of fiction, consisting of three distinct and unconnected tales which may be published either together as a work of 3 vols. . . . or separately as single vols. as shall deemed most advisable.

All three had put their hearts and minds into furthering their chances to become paid authors. Even after having learned how difficult finding a publisher could be, they pressed on undaunted.

THE BELL BROTHERS

For their next works, the three women chose to write in the literary form most popular in Victorian England: the novel. The novel had gained attention in the eighteenth century, popularized by authors such as Daniel Defoe and Henry Fielding. Its popularity—and its literary reputation—skyrocketed in the first half of the nineteenth century, mostly because of the highly acclaimed writings of Sir Walter Scott. Several female authors also achieved success as novelists. Jane Austen's *Pride and Prejudice* (1813), *Emma* (1816), and other tales were considered the best in the genre of "comedy of manners," and Mary Shelley's *Frankenstein* (1818) was a wildly popular example of the Gothic genre of novel.

However, it was still much easier for a man to have his work published, so the Brontë sisters did not waver from their decision to remain Currer, Ellis, and Acton Bell to the world.

The novel Charlotte began working on, *The Professor*, tells the story of a young Englishwoman in Brussels and her relationship with her teacher. It is a fictionalized account of Charlotte's relationship with Constantin Héger, but with a happier ending. The novel displayed enlightened views of equality for women long before there was any organized women's movement.

Anne's novel, *Agnes Grey*, can also be described as autobiographical. It is the story of a governess who falls in love with and later marries a young curate. Like Anne, Agnes is deeply attached to family and home, but she knows she must leave in order to make her own way in life. She embarks upon a career that requires all her energy and strength with only her sense of duty and her religious beliefs to sustain her. Unlike Anne, who kept her love for Willie Weightman a secret, Agnes finds fulfillment in her marriage. The story is simply written and has a happy ending, such as Anne might have wished for her own life.

Emily's *Wuthering Heights* was very different in content and scope from the other two works. The story, influenced by Gothic horror tales, was so wild and fierce that it almost frightened Charlotte. The powerful characters, Cathy and Heathcliff, have been immortalized in the literary world and are still legendary as a famous romantic couple. The description of the landscape of the windswept moors is the finest in English literature. The moods and seasons are painted in short, vivid, extremely beautiful passages.

With each novel completed, the sisters set upon the hard work of marketing their manuscripts. For a year and a half, they sent out packages only to have them returned again and again. Finally, *Wuthering Heights* and *Agnes Grey* were accepted by T. C. Newby, a minor publisher in London. Newby agreed to publish the two titles in one volume and charged the authors £50. Charlotte was happy for her sisters but disappointed that her book had not been placed.

Thoughts of manuscript submissions were put on hold for a few months while Charlotte accompanied her father to Manchester, where he was to undergo cataract surgery. A sooty, smoke-filled industrial city, Manchester was not a pleasant place to stay. But Charlotte once again had to shoulder the responsibility and duty, and she found lodging rooms for them to stay in while her father recuperated.

Her isolation in Manchester, as her father convalesced in a darkened upstairs room, gave her the opportunity to begin a second novel. While she had been somewhat hesitant in writing *The Professor*, since it contained much of her own personal heartache, such was not the case with this book, *Jane*

Eyre. The fully fictitious nature of the story gave her freedom, and her pen fairly flew as she wrote page after page. This story of a governess who was poor and plain yet strong of character—and about her tempestuous relationship with her employer, Mr. Rochester—would become one of the most famous in Victorian England.

Upon Charlotte's return to Haworth with her father, whose operation was a success, the manuscript of *The Professor* found its way back home once again. However, this time, the reader at Smith, Elder & Company in London expressed his interest in seeing more of her work—specifically a novel in three parts, should she decide to write one. Three-volume works happened to be the fashion, and that exactly described Charlotte's work in progress. She hurriedly finished the novel and mailed it to the attention of William Smith Williams, the man who had signed the letter to her.

When *Jane Eyre* arrived at the office of Smith, Elder, Williams read it and was mesmerized. He quickly put it in the hands of the owner of the publishing company, George Murray Smith. Smith received it on a Saturday, took it home late that night, and decided to read it the next morning after breakfast. When his carriage arrived at his front door to take him to a noon appointment, he sent it away. He read throughout the day, finishing the manuscript before going to bed that night. "The next day," Smith would later write, "we wrote to 'Currer Bell' accepting the book for publication."

George Smith had reason beyond literary quality for accepting Charlotte's manuscript. A young man who had taken over his father's business, Smith was struggling through hard times. He had learned that his father's former partner, Mr. Elder, had embezzled funds and put the company on a rocky road full of financial problems. Currer Bell's book, as Smith saw it, could very well solve those problems. It turned out he was right.

From that moment, a series of events happened in a whirlwind. The proofs of the novel were in Charlotte's hands in September 1847, and the book appeared in print October 16—amazingly quick for that day and age. Enthusiastic reviews began pouring in as *Jane Eyre* seized the attention of Victorian England. The *Westminster Review* wrote, "Decidedly the best novel of the year." A leading critic, G. H. Lewes, who would later correspond with Charlotte, wrote, "This indeed is a book after our own heart . . . no such book has gladdened our eyes for a long while. . . . The story is not only of singular interest . . . but fastens itself upon your attention, and will not leave you."

Newby, meanwhile was dallying with the manuscripts of Ellis and Acton Bell. But once he saw the popularity of the novel from Currer Bell, he realized he had something big on his hands. In December, as *Jane Eyre* moved into a second printing, Newby brought out *Wuthering Heights* and *Agnes Grey*. The works were not well produced; they were hurriedly and carelessly done and full of printer's errors. Neither book met with many favorable reviews. While Acton Bell's book was described as insipid, Ellis Bell's was considered the product of a dogged, brutal, and morose mind.

In the nineteenth century, many critics believed that the purpose of a novel was to uplift the soul or teach a social lesson. Anything that smacked of coarseness was met with disdain. Some reviewers objected to the "demonic" influences they detected in *Wuthering Heights*, particularly the vengeful and amoral character of Heathcliff. Thus, the unfavorable reviews had more to do with content than writing style. Meanwhile, rumors flitted around London as to the gender and identities of the authors named Bell. Were they related, or were they all one and the same person?

In spite of public reaction, all three sisters planned to begin subsequent works. Charlotte noted later that her two sisters were ready to try again. However, if Emily did begin a second work, there is no record of it. Charlotte worked on *Shirley*, while Anne wrote *The Tenant of Wildfell Hall*. Anne's second book was radically different from her first. Drawing on her painful observations of Branwell's deterioration, she told an unsparing tale of a naïve woman driven to desperation by her drunken and debauched husband. Its darkness of theme mirrored Emily's *Wuthering Heights*, although, unlike that work, the book condemns evil behavior.

Charlotte suggested to Anne that she send her second work to Smith, Elder, where she would be treated with more kindness, but Anne refused. Newby brought out the book in June 1848. In a totally unscrupulous manner, he advertised the book so as to imply it was by the same author as *Wuthering Heights* and *Jane Eyre*. Newby even offered the book to an American publishing house, stating that he had Currer Bell's next novel.

When the firm of Smith, Elder heard this news they were fairly livid. Calmly, they wrote to Currer Bell for a clear explanation. When Charlotte received the letter she was shocked to think they suspected her of evil dealings. The only remedy, as she could see it, would be for the sisters to travel to London to reveal their identities in person. Emily would have none of it and flatly refused to go with them. Not only did she not want to leave home, she was adamant that her identity be kept secret. Charlotte and Anne had no choice but to respect her wishes.

By this time, Charlotte had admitted to her father that she had published a novel. She read him some of the good reviews, then invited him to read the novel. After he read it, he came to tea and said to Emily and Anne, "Girls, do you know Charlotte has been writing a book, and it is much better than likely?" Branwell, on the other hand, was told nothing of his sisters' successful ventures. They feared that in his condition such knowledge would be too much for him.

On their trip to London, Charlotte and Anne became acquainted with William Smith Williams, the reader for Smith, Elder, and George Smith, both of whom would become longtime friends of Charlotte's. The social whirl of the huge city, to which the sisters were totally unaccustomed, wearied them greatly. Upon arriving back home, Charlotte wrote to Mary Taylor in New Zealand (who knew the secret of the Bell Brothers):

> . . . A more jaded wretch than I looked when I returned it would be difficult to conceive. I was thin when I went, but was meagre indeed when I returned; my face looked grey and very old, with strange, deep lines ploughed in it; my eyes stared unnaturally. I was weak and yet restless. In a while, however, the bad effects of excitement went off and I regained my normal condition.

Charlotte was fated to always have such reactions to being out in public; at times she became physically ill and unable to eat. She would never completely overcome this painful shyness.

Even though only a few knew the true identities of the Bell brothers, it was a certainty that they were now well-established authors. Charlotte's *Jane Eyre* was immensely popular, and although Anne's two novels and Emily's *Wuthering Heights* had received generally hostile reviews, the books were selling fairly well. After Mr. Brontë went to bed each evening, the three would gather around the dining room table and write. They read passages aloud to one another, asking for advice and sharing thoughts and reactions. No more would there ever be talk of taking on the hated position of governess, nor of starting a school in order to make a living. It looked as though the sisters were on their way to the prosperity, success, and happiness that had eluded them for so long.

TRAGEDY UPON TRAGEDY

Unfortunately, extended happiness eluded the Brontë family. Branwell's condition was deteriorating. He somehow kept obtaining money to purchase a little gin to get him through another day. Then his nights were filled with nightmares, causing him to thrash about in his sleep and cry out in agony. His debts piled up, and his sisters were forced to pay them. Finally, tuberculosis, the scourge of the town of Haworth, took hold of his already emaciated body. He died on September 24, 1848, at the age of 31. Charlotte, angry at him up until the end, was able to forgive him before he died.

Soon after Branwell's death, Charlotte became violently ill, perhaps due to her feelings of guilt at the anger she had harbored toward her brother. When her father needed her the most, she for the first time was unable to rally to his side. She felt shame in the midst of terrible grief, and her anger was not aimed solely at Branwell, but also at her father, who had shown his son so much favor. In a letter to Williams, who had become a close friend, she admitted, "My poor father naturally thought more of his *only* son than of his daughters, and, much and long as he had suffered on his account, he cried out for his loss like David for that of Absalom—my son! my son!—and refused at first to be comforted." Charlotte's illness lingered, and with it she suffered a depression that would not allow her to write.

Branwell's funeral took place on a day of cold east winds and soaking rain. Emily followed the casket through the graveyard to the church in the cold rain and sat in the damp, icy church through the service. She caught a cold that she could not shake. October continued with an icy chill, and the sounds of Emily's fitful coughing filled the house. Whenever she moved quickly, she caught her breath suddenly and grabbed at her heart, betraying a sharp pain in her chest. The symptoms terrified Charlotte and Anne. But worse than the symptoms was the fact that Emily refused to admit to her illness. She stoically went about her work, though she could barely drag herself out of bed each morning. In the evenings she sat before the fire with her needlework in her lap, but stared into space, her hands idle.

Emily had never needed any other person during her life. She was complete within herself. Now she needed no one in her time of death. She refused all help from her sisters or from the medical profession. Whether her seeming willingness to embrace death was due to her deep grief over losing Branwell or the disappointment of the continuing negative reviews of her book, no one will ever know. Trying to compete with Charlotte's overwhelming literary success could not have been easy. Slowly, right before their eyes, Emily slipped away from her family. She died on December 18, just a few months after they had buried Branwell.

Charlotte went through Emily's things after her death. In her desk box were several clippings of reviews of *Wuthering Heights*, some praising Currer at the expense of Ellis. While outwardly Emily may have appeared aloof and unshaken, perhaps beneath it all she was far from indifferent.

Shortly after Emily's passing, Charlotte looked at Anne and noticed with horror that her surviving sister was also not at all well. The little cough began just as Emily's had. Soon Anne was sitting before the fire rocking absently, too listless to write, read, or even talk. Considering the poor hygiene practices in their day, and the fact that Emily and Anne had shared a bedroom and a bed, it is not surprising that both should have the same disease. Unlike Emily, Anne willingly admitted she was ill and agreed to any and all treatments. She also talked to Charlotte about the illness, so Charlotte did not feel the agony of forced neglect that she'd experienced with Emily. Unfortunately, the medical treatments of the day were mostly useless: blisters (hot compresses), cod-liver oil, carbonate of iron, draftless rooms, and a respirator.

As her health failed, Anne's heart and mind turned to a place where she had been truly happy—at Scarborough near the sea. She had spent several summers there with the Robinson family during her stint as a governess. She asked Charlotte to help her return one more time. At first Charlotte balked, knowing Anne could not possibly survive the trip. She held out hope that with the coming of spring, Anne might be somewhat better. Then they could travel in the warmer months. But when spring came, Anne was no better. Finally, Charlotte gave in and rented rooms in Scarborough. Mr. Brontë agreed that Charlotte could leave him. Ellen was to meet them and help Charlotte care for the ailing Anne.

Anne was happy to be at Scarborough once more, and her spirits were briefly revived. Charlotte and Ellen took her out in a donkey cart along the beach, and one day she even felt well enough to walk alone. After that, her strength quickly ebbed. On the morning of May 28, 1849, she died with Charlotte and Ellen close by. Writing to Williams at Smith, Elder, Charlotte described Anne's passing:

> Let me now add that she died without severe struggle, resigned, trusting in God—thankful for release from a suffering life— deeply assured that a better existence lay before her. . . . Anne, from her childhood, seemed preparing for an early death. Emily's spirit seemed strong enough to bear her to fullness of years. They are both gone, and so is poor Branwell, and Papa has now me only—the weakest, puniest, least promising of his six children. Consumption has taken the whole five.

Charlotte went on to explain that she buried Anne at Scarborough to save her father the further grief of a third funeral. However, her decision may have been financial as well, since it would have cost a great deal to have the body taken back to Haworth. Sadly, she returned to her father, the servants Tabby and Martha, and Emily's dogs. The dogs, she told Ellen in a letter, were in a state of ecstasy, no doubt certain that Charlotte's arrival meant the other two sisters would soon follow. If Haworth had felt like a prison before, it now seemed even more so to Charlotte. Crushing loneliness and sorrow gripped her.

To his credit, Mr. Brontë, always a crusader for just causes, got up a petition to the General Board of Health about the intolerable conditions at Haworth. The findings of a subsequent inspection were ghastly. One grim discovery was that the pump in the parsonage's kitchen drew water from a well dug just a few yards from the cemetery.

By this time, Smith, Elder had grown anxious and impatient for another book from their star author. It wasn't good business to let the public wait too long. Both Williams and Smith kept up a steady flow of letters and parcels of books to the Haworth parsonage. But Charlotte could not be hurried. She wrote only under inspiration, she explained to them in her most dignified manner. She could scarcely understand how Charles Dickens, the most esteemed male novelist of that era, could turn out multitudes of stories on demand.

Whereas before the three sisters drew strength from one another as they wrote, now Charlotte was totally alone. She could not bring herself to talk to her father about either the writing process or about her successes. Her novel in progress, *Shirley*, had become even more difficult to write because the main character was a likeness of Emily. The story highlighted an incident in England's recent past, when workmen smashed machines in the woolen mills out of frustration from losing jobs and income to the Industrial Revolution. She'd heard the stories from her father in her childhood.

Upon publication, *Shirley* brought good reviews, although not as wildly enthusiastic as those for *Jane Eyre*. With the release of this novel, yet another with a female heroine, suspicions about the true identity of Currer Bell began to surface. Even Charlotte's friend Ellen began to ask questions. Eventually, the full truth came out. Charlotte shuddered to think of it, since she had never sought fame or glory. On the other hand, it gave her the opportunity to meet and mix with the literary community, as she'd often longed to do. Eventually she emerged more and more from her quiet existence into the outside world, although she was never quite comfortable with it.

Charlotte was to pay five visits to London, each one a mix of excitement and intense strain. Her publisher arranged special outings to art galleries and the theater. She met the literary giants of her time, including numerous literary critics, the writers Elizabeth Cleghorn Gaskell and Harriet Martineau, and her idol, the popular novelist William Makepeace Thackeray. Elizabeth Gaskell would later become her biographer. Unlike other women writers of her day, Mrs. Gaskell was married with children. She often invited Charlotte to stay as a guest in the Gaskells' large house outside

Manchester. Although Charlotte was never fond of small children, she became especially drawn to Mrs. Gaskell's children and enjoyed the Gaskells' happy family life.

During every visit to London, the young, handsome George Smith paid close attention to Charlotte, so much so that she mistook his affection to be more than businesslike courtesy. For a time, she entertained the idea that he might propose marriage to her. He never did. (Years later, Smith admitted he was never in love with Charlotte.) Once again, Charlotte had to suffer in silence, keeping her emotions buried deep within her heart. George was married to another in 1853.

Back at Haworth, Charlotte began her next novel, *Villette*. This book must have greatly surprised the editors at Smith, Elder. Some of the characters closely resembled George Smith and his mother, in whose home Charlotte had stayed many times. *Villette* also drew upon her Belgium experiences, which she had previously used in her unpublished novel, *The Professor*. The main character of *Villette*, Lucy Snowe, is torn between her attraction to her teacher, an analogue of M. Héger, and young Graham Bretton, the character based on George Smith. Published in January 1853, *Villette* drew critical acclaim. Author George Eliot—another famous female novelist with a male pen name—wrote to a friend, " 'Villette,' 'Villette,'—have you read it? . . . I am only just returning to a sense of the real world about me, for I have been reading 'Villette,' a still more wonderful book than 'Jane Eyre.' There is something preternatural in its power."

With the novel out of the way and George Smith married, the loneliness of Haworth must have been more acute than ever for Charlotte. After she'd sent off the manuscript, Charlotte happened to notice her father's curate, the Reverend Arthur Bell Nicholls, acting rather strangely. He seemed to become extremely nervous when he was near her or when he tried to talk to her. Eventually, he revealed that he had loved Charlotte Brontë for some time and now wished her to be his wife.

While Charlotte did not love Nicholls, she was quite lonely. She felt she should give herself a chance at least to get to know him better. Mr. Nicholls' persistence paid off. The two were married on June 29, 1854, over the strong objections of Charlotte's father, who called Nicholls a penniless opportunist hoping to better himself by marrying the famous Brontë daughter. Mr. Brontë, who'd long been accustomed to Charlotte's attentive care, was not willing to give her up. Though he begrudgingly gave permission for the marriage, he did not attend the wedding.

Only on their honeymoon journey to Nicholls' home in Ireland did Charlotte come to really know her husband. She learned he came from a fine, loving home with a large extended family. All of his relatives assured her that she'd married a wonderful man. Charlotte's life changed after marriage as she became absorbed in her husband's work. Always an attentive, caring curate, Nicholls was concerned about all his parishioners. Soon there were teas and various meetings at the parsonage, whereas previously guests were rare. Even though she was busier than ever, Charlotte began a new novel entitled *Emma*.

In November 1854, Charlotte became ill after a long walk with Arthur during which it began to rain and Charlotte became soaking wet. She had already begun to surmise she might be pregnant. Now, her nausea was combined with a bad cold and a cough that she could not shake. In spite of the fact that a doctor pronounced her illness not fatal, she continued to weaken. She eventually fell into a delirium and died March 31, 1855. Charlotte was buried next to her mother, her sisters, and her brother.

Toward the end, Charlotte had written to Ellen to say that her husband was a caring, loving nurse to her throughout her illness. She truly did come to love him. True to Charlotte's wishes, Arthur Nicholls remained in the parsonage to care for her elderly father. The two lived in the same house but separately, in a strangely aloof relationship. Mr. Brontë died in 1861, after which Nicholls returned to Ireland to live out the rest of his life. He later married a cousin, but he never forgot his dear Charlotte.

After Charlotte's death, Patrick Brontë became increasingly concerned about his daughter's fame. The death of Currer Bell had unleashed a flurry of publicity about the author, much of it erroneous. Mr. Brontë felt that the truth must be recorded and published. He contacted Mrs. Gaskell and requested that she research Charlotte's life and write her biography

While Mrs. Gaskell omitted information that she thought to be harmful to Charlotte's reputation, she told the story with deep respect and keen insight. *The Life of Charlotte Brontë*, published by Smith, Elder was an instant success. It remains an important source of information on the famous writer and her family.

The publishing house also chose to print *The Professor* in 1857. The unfinished *Emma* was published in fragment form in George Smith's *Cornhill Magazine* in the spring of 1860. The story bears similarities to *Jane Eyre*, but one can only guess where it might have gone had Charlotte lived to finish it.

Ellen Nussey devoted the rest of her life to Charlotte's memory, sharing letters and reminiscences with all who were interested. She lived to be 80 years old.

The parsonage was opened as a museum in 1928 and is still visited by thousands of sightseers every year. The museum displays articles of clothing, jewelry, writing materials, books, and even the manuscripts and drawings created by the Brontë children.

The Brontë works, particularly *Jane Eyre* and *Wuthering Heights*, would eventually become ranked among the world's classics. Each succeeding generation discovers afresh these powerful stories set in the sweeping Yorkshire moors, never tiring of their timeless treatment of love, passion, destiny, and undying courage. The novels had a tremendous influence on subsequent writers and stood as proof that women were just as capable as men of producing great literature. Perhaps Emily Brontë would be pleased to know that the much-maligned *Wuthering Heights* is now considered by many scholars the most sophisticated of all the family's works, anticipating the darker, more fatalistic tone of late Victorian and early twentieth-century novels by decades.

Stage, radio, and television plays about the Brontës abound, as do motion picture presentations of their novels and fresh editions of the novels themselves. Though the lives of the Brontë sisters were short, their talent succeeded in giving them immortality.

Examining the Novels of the Brontë Sisters

A young girl arrives at a mysterious mansion to work as a governess, where she finds herself attracted to the head of the manor, Edward Rochester. While she fights this attraction, she notices odd occurrences in the home: a crackling laugh that echoes through the empty hallways, a bed mysteriously lit on fire, and an attic floor shut off from the rest of the household. Yet, amidst the strange events, the young girl cannot ignore her growing love for Rochester, and passion eventually wins. When she becomes engaged to the man, it appears as if her story is destined to become a happily-ever-after love story. But on the day of her wedding, she discovers the horrible truth: Her husband-to-be is already married, and his insane wife is living in the attic.

This story might easily be mistaken as one designed for a lesser medium, the television mini-drama, but it is in fact the story of Jane Eyre, the young heroine of the nineteenth-century novel of the same name. Penned by Charlotte Brontë, *Jane Eyre* was considered a success by the reading public when it was published in 1847. The same year, *Wuthering Heights*, by Charlotte's sister Emily, and *Agnes Grey*, by the youngest Brontë sister, Anne, were both published. Thus, the careers of one of the most influential literary families in the history of English literature began. *Wuthering Heights* and *Jane Eyre* are still two of the most widely read British classics today, and Charlotte Brontë's other novels, *Shirley*, *Villette*, and *The Professor*, have also gained recent acclaim. Anne Brontë, usually considered the "unknown Brontë sister," has herself undergone more recent scrutiny. In the past, her novels, *The Tenant of Wildfell Hall*, and the aforementioned *Agnes Grey*, lacked the popularity of her sisters' works, but recently they have gained new respect. In 1930, George Moore even said that if Anne Brontë had lived longer, this "literary Cinderella" may have taken a place beside Jane Austen.[1]

The Brontë novels, published between the years 1847 and 1853 (*The Professor* was published posthumously in 1857) were written at a time of literary greatness in British history. Jane Austen's novels and Mary Shelley's *Frankenstein* had already been introduced to the reading public, while Charles Dickens and William Thackeray were at their peak in popularity. These writers were entering an age in which they wanted to examine the social issues of their era, but they were often drawn to another, earlier time. In an era that encompassed both progress and chaos, critic Maggie Berg explains, "The Victorians were in a double bind. They wanted truth, but too much of it could be disturbing."[2] The Victorians, while embracing both the present and the future, were also drawn to the past, and thus the influence of the literary genres of the past can be seen in the Brontë works. Yet, it is clear that the Brontë sisters, even though they were seemingly sheltered from the rest of the world by the seclusion of the Yorkshire moors, were interested in the changing world around them.

LITERARY INFLUENCES: THE INFLUENCE OF GOTHIC NOVELS AND THE BYRONIC HERO

The spirit of Catherine haunts the opening pages of Emily Brontë's *Wuthering Heights*, while the heroine in Charlotte's *Jane Eyre* encounters mysterious, ghostly happenings at the mansion where she is working as a governess. Anyone who ventures into the world of the Brontës will immediately recognize the influence of the gothic. Crumbling castles, ghostly figures, supernatural events, and bleak graveyards all lurk in the gothic novel. Behind these images are the recurring themes of suppressed sexual longing and forbidden love. Horace Walpole is traditionally given credit for originating the gothic genre with his novel, *The Castle of Otranto*, published in 1764. The novel's success spurred other gothic works. Today, books referred to as belonging to the gothic tradition include Matthew Lewis's *The Monk* (1795), Ann Radcliffe's *Mysteries of Udolpho* (1794), and Mary Shelley's *Frankenstein* (1818). American writers who owe a debt to the gothic style include Nathaniel Hawthorne and Edgar Allen Poe, along with many contemporary authors, including Stephen King.

The heroine takes a special place in gothic novels. She must not only venture into dangerous escapades to face mysterious, often frightening, circumstances. She must also fight the role in which society has placed her:

a submissive woman who relies only on men for both her personal safety and her very existence. According to critic Ellen Moers, Ann Radcliffe was formative in popularizing the gothic heroine:

> For Mrs. Radcliffe, the Gothic novel was a device to send maidens on distant and exciting journeys without offending the proprieties. In the power of villains, her heroines are forced to do what they could never do alone, whatever their ambitions: scurry up the top of pasteboard Alps, spy out exotic vistas, penetrate bandit-infested forests. And indoors, inside Mrs. Radcliffe's castles, her heroines can scuttle miles along corridors, descend into dungeons, and explore secret chambers without a chaperone, because the Gothic castle, however much in ruins, is still an indoor and therefore freely female space.[3]

In *Shirley*, a young girl reading Radcliffe's *The Italian* tells Caroline Helstone that the book makes her "long to travel" because "in reading it you feel as if you were far away from England" (299). This young woman wants to escape England because she fears the suffocation of the world around her. She simply does not want a life like Caroline's life: " I am resolved that my life shall be a life. Not a black trance like the toad's buried in marble; nor a long slow death like yours in Briarfield rectory" (299). This young woman sees England as a trap from which the only escape is to physically journey to another world. In her mind, staying to fight the boredom or entrapment of society around her is not an option.

This journey motif is found in many of the Brontë novels. The heroines are not looking for adventure; rather, they are seeking a way to escape their oppressive lives. Through this escape, they are able to explore worlds outside their boundaries. Both Jane Eyre and Lucy Snowe are orphans and unloved; their journeys lead them to take positions as teachers and governesses, where they experience not only supernatural occurrences but also love and adventure. To help her poor family, Agnes Grey also leaves her home to take on the position of governess, and in *The Tenant of Wildfell Hall*, Anne Brontë uses the journey motif to explain how Helen Huntingdon escapes her abusive husband.

The Ann Radcliffe gothic heroine, although taking on adventurous roles, seldom has to deal with real-life traumatic experiences. She fights her oppressive background and wins. She conquers the hero and her frightening surroundings with ease, seldom suffering more than a few scrapes and bruises. Radcliffe is often cited as the most influential writer of the gothic heroine, but this heroine, in essence, is examined and dismissed by the

Brontës. The Brontës, explains Diane Long Hoeveler, "rewrote gothic feminism for a newly emerging bourgeois class of women: governesses and wives and mothers responsible for the education as well as their charges."[4] In the character of Catherine Earnshaw, Emily Brontë created a "a gothic feminist" who is torn "between her own nature and her own best social, economic, political interests, her own impulses, and her own survival."[5] Catherine is welcomed into the Linton home where she is enticed into a world that seems safe compared with the mysteries of the moors and the passionate but sometimes frightening love of her beloved Heathcliff. She is temporarily won over by this world, for she marries Edward Linton, neglecting Heathcliff with the infamous words, "It would degrade me to marry Heathcliff, now; so he shall never know how I love him; and that, not because he's handsome, Nelly, but because he's more myself than I am. Whatever our souls are made of, his and mine are [the] same" (86). Catherine marries a man who is presumably safe, but unlike the gothic heroines of the Radcliffe novels, Emily Brontë's heroine is forced "to actually live with her weak husband and actually become pregnant, and the indignity of childbirth is not suffered lightly by most gothic feminists."[6]

This same subversion of the Radcliffe gothic heroine is also seen in Charlotte Brontë's novels, for "Jane Eyre appears to be the only gothic feminist who survives childbirth and lives with her gothic hero to tell the tale, but as everyone knows her gothic hero has been tamed and ritualistically wounded."[7] When Rochester attempts to save his first wife from the fire that destroys his home, he is blinded, and it is only through Jane's love that his eyesight is restored. *The Tenant of Wildfell Hall* also dismisses the traditional gothic heroine. Helen Huntingdon is introduced in the novel as a woman who is "clad in black" with "raven black hair disposed in black ringlets" and eyes "concealed by their drooping lids" and " long black lashes" (17). Certainly, such a description characterizes a gothic woman of mystery, but her secret is more than mysterious. It is truly frightening: she is fleeing from an abusive husband. In Anne Brontë's novel, Helen does try to redeem her abusive husband, but eventually she is forced to flee from him, thus failing where a gothic heroine always succeeds—in taming the mysterious and dark lover.

The other gothic elements found in the Brontë novels—old mansions, supernatural spirits, and dark graveyards—undergo a transformation similar to the Radcliffe gothic heroine. Robert Heilman explains that Charlotte Brontë creates a "New Gothic" in her work by revising familiar gothic images to create "new ways to achieve the ends served by old gothic."[8] The supernatural and gothic elements are not placed in her works to create ghost stories. For example, in *Jane Eyre*, Heilman notes, "Jane's strange, fearful symbolic dreams are not mere thrillers but reflect the tensions of the engagement period, the stress of the wedding day debate with Rochester, and the longing for Rochester after she has left him."[9] In *Villette*, a ghostly nun appears to Lucy several times throughout the novel. The ghost is more than just a symbol of terror. Heilman explains that the first appearance is a mere product of Lucy's own disabling mental state, but another appearance by the nun, also witnessed by Paul, represents the "inseparable bond" of the two lovers.[10]

Emily Brontë also challenges the role of traditional gothic elements. Nicholas Marsh, in comparing *Wuthering Heights* with *The Monk*, declares that while Lewis uses his written images to try to convince the reader that the supernatural events taking place in his novel are real, Emily Brontë never wants the reader to really believe in the existence of her ghost. Instead, she ties her gothic symbols of ghostly visions to questions of "psychology and obsession."[11] The reader may readily attribute the ghost to Heathcliff's obsessive love for Catherine, but seldom does the reader really dwell on the question of the ghost's actual existence.

Although Anne Brontë is not usually acknowledged as readily influenced by the gothic genre, gothic elements can nevertheless also be seen in her two novels, especially in *The Tenant of Wildfell Hall*. Critic Bettina Knapp explains that the architectural constructs and landscapes used to create the sense of mystery found in the works of Ann Radcliffe are also found in the depiction of Wildfell Hall and its surroundings.[12] These same constructs are also in *Agnes Grey;* while the novel seemingly wants to focus on the idea of social justice in the role of the governess, the gothic landscape is also present. In both novels, the place where the young heroine acts as governess is a mansion, complete with long dark passageways and rooms at the top of back stairways. The heroines in Anne Brontë's novels do have to deal with abuse from the world around them; however, such gothic settings help empower them to conquer the social constrictions.

Besides the gothic elements, the image of the Byronic hero is perhaps the most widely recognized Romantic element seen in the Brontë novels. The Byronic hero, who emerged from the eighteenth-century writing of Lord Bryon, is not characterized by his virtue and bravery. Instead, he is often dark and mysterious, often violent and cruel, and almost never handsome—at least not in the traditional sense. The influence of such a hero is clear in the Brontës' works, especially in *Jane Eyre* and *Wuthering Heights.* Rochester, with his "colorless, olive face, square, massive brow, broad and jetty eyebrows, deep eyes, strong features, firm, grim mouth," and Heathcliff, who is described as a "dirty, ragged black-haired child" in his youth and who grows up to be a "dark haired gypsy," are not handsome men.

Furthermore, they cannot be described as the romantic gentlemen of novels past. Rochester mocks Jane, telling her bluntly that she is not pretty, while Heathcliff, after the death of his beloved Catherine, brutalizes all around him.

The Byronic hero does not disappear in the other Brontë novels. Lucy Snowe's true love, M. Paul, is described as a "little man of unreasonable moods," who is prone to jealousy that "was not tender jealousy of the heart, but that sterner, narrower sentiment, whose seat is in the heart" (334). The main character in *The Professor*, the only one of Charlotte Brontë's stories told from a male point of view, is also far from what might be considered an ideal hero. Upon meeting the young student he would marry at the end of the novel, he dismisses her coldly: "You have come in too late to receive a lesson to-day; try to be more punctual next time" (91). And both of the men in Helen Huntingdon's life should be considered Byronic heroes. Arthur Huntingdon is a womanizing drunk whose lifestyle eventually kills him, and while Gilbert Markham seems to be a saint compared with Helen's brutal first husband, several passages in the novel suggest that he too has a dark side, a side that is revealed when he attacks Mr. Lawrence for no apparent reason.

Clearly, the Brontë sisters were influenced by the gothic genre. Their Byronic heroes, gothic heroines, and supernatural and mysterious images haunt the pages of their works. However, a closer look at the Victorian era and the society the sisters lived in reveal that they were influenced by more than just the past.

THE BRONTË NOVELS AND "THE WOMAN QUESTION"

The novels of the Brontë sisters exhibit influences from Romanticism and gothic genres, but in many ways they clearly fit into the realm of the Victorian novel, which often struggled to examine the social issues of a rapidly changing British society. The beginning of the 1800s marked a progressive, yet troubled time in Great Britain. London became one of the most influential cities in the world. The population grew from 2 million to 6.5 million by the end of the 1800s and reflected the change from individual land ownership and farming in rural settings to manufacturing in urban factories. This Industrial Revolution made England a rich country, but the rapid growth also brought its own share of woes. In the 1840s, economic depression and fear of unemployment lead to widespread unrest and rioting, a tale that is addressed in Charlotte Brontë's *Shirley*.

Unemployment, however, was not the only growing pain that Victorian society suffered, and many Victorian novelists of the time explored other issues of England's new society. Charles Kingsley, in *Alton Locke*, exposed the scandal of London's poor sanitation systems, while Elizabeth Gaskell, in *North and South*, explored the deplorable working conditions of the industrial mills. Charles Dickens, through his many works including *Oliver Twist*, examined the problems of child labor and poverty.

The Victorian era was a time when many of the traditional roles of women were readily being questioned. With more and more women entering the workplace in factories, their role as wife and mother was disrupted. Victorians named this confusion "The Woman Question." The Woman Question explored issues of sexual inequality in politics, economic life, education, and social settings. Feminists not only fought for women's right to vote, but they also fought for reform in the workplace and in educational institutions. But reform was not an easy process, as Victorian feminists found out, and to make the Woman Question even more complex, Victorian feminists were themselves split on many of the issues. Leading the confusion was Queen Victoria herself, who was a strong supporter of women's education and even helped establish a college for women, but was against giving women the right to vote, calling the suffrage campaign "a mad folly."

Marriage was one of the key concerns of Victorian feminists. Most Victorians advocated marriage as an important part of Victorian society, but feminists were very much aware that marriage could be far from the ideal situation for a woman. Marriage is a prominent symbol in Victorian novels written by women at the time, including those of George Eliot and Jane Austen, so it should not be surprising that marriage figures prominently in all the Brontë novels. With the exception of *Villette*, all the novels end with marriage. Agnes Grey marries Edward Weston, and Helen Huntingdon, after her first husband dies, marries Gilbert Markham. Jane Eyre marries Rochester, and William Crimsworth marries Frances Henri, and, despite many concerns and worries, the two heroines of *Shirley* marry: Caroline Helstone marries Robert Moore and Shirley Keeler marries Louis Moore. And amidst the tortured romance of Heathcliff and Catherine in *Wuthering Heights* lies a story focused on marriage: Catherine marries Edgar Linton, while Heathcliff marries Isabella Linton. The novel also details the marriages of the next generation: young Catherine marries Linton, Heathcliff's son. After young Linton's death, the novel ends with young Catherine and Hareton, the son of Hindley, planning a future together.

The Brontë sisters seemed to be well aware that marriage could be a prison for many women. While Victorian society dictated that women be caretakers and queens of their own homes, Victorian law did little to protect women's rights in marriage. In a marriage, a woman could be physically and emotionally abused and powerless to walk away. A man had full rights to his wife's money. Anne Brontë was well aware of the injustices of British law, as demonstrated by *The Tenant of Wildfell Hall*, in which the young heroine is forced to hide from her abusive, alcoholic husband. *Wuthering Heights* can also be seen as an exposition of what happens when women are trapped in abusive marriages. When Heathcliff is denied the chance to live his life with Catherine, he marries Isabella, who tolerates his abuse. And in *Shirley*, young Shirley fears marriage because "I could never be my own mistress more. A terrible thought! It suffocates me! Nothing irks me like the idea of being a burden and a bore—a inevitable burden, a ceaseless bore" (161). To Shirley, marriage not only limits a woman's freedom, but also burdens the husband.

Yet, while the trappings of marriage can be seen in these works, the Brontë sisters refuse to let their heroines become victims. The Brontës want their characters to marry out of choice, not out of necessity. Financial dependence was one reason many women were encouraged to marry, but as, Patricia Beers points out, "Charlotte Brontë's heroines are not compelled to fall back on marriage for financial independence; she takes care to provide for them first."[13] Jane Eyre, although poor for most of her life, is left a fortune before she returns to Rochester. Shirley Keelder is rich from the start of the novel.

Money does not seem to be in the picture in Anne Brontë's novels, for her heroines marry for reasons of love, instead of necessity. Agnes Grey marries a man who clearly cannot offer her material wealth. And in *The Tenant of Wildfell Hall*, Anne Brontë refuses to let a young, 25-year-old widow mourn the death of a worthless, alcoholic husband. As W.A. Craik points out, "To have her not marry again would be the sentimental, conventional ending, so uncongenial to Anne Brontë."[14]

Employment, another concern for Victorian feminists, was considered out of the question for most women, yet a surplus of women in the 1800s meant that many were left without men to care for them. Job opportunities were sparse. Only "unrespectable" women worked in the factories, and thus the only "respectable" jobs were those of governess and teacher. Rarely were any of these coveted positions, as the Brontë sisters themselves found out. All the sisters attended boarding schools, and both Charlotte and Emily taught while Anne served as governess for two families. It is readily evident that their experiences were the basis of many of their novels. For example, through the eyes of Charlotte's little Jane Eyre, the boarding school to which she is sent is described:

> Our clothing was insufficient to protect us from the severe cold:
> we had no boots, the snow got into our shoes and melted there;

our ungloved hands became numbed and covered with chilblains,
as were our feet: I remember well the distracting irritation I
endured from this cause, every evening when my feet inflamed;
and the torture of thrusting the swelled, raw stiff toes into my
shoes in the morning. Then the scanty supply of food was
distressing: with the keen appetites of growing children, we had
scarcely sufficient to keep alive a delicate invalid. From this
deficiency of nourishment resulted an abuse, which pressed
hardly on the younger pupils; whenever the famished great girls
had an opportunity, they would coax or menace the little ones
out of their portion. (69)

This school, where little Jane Eyre loses her best friend to malaria, is in
all probability based on the school where the two oldest Brontë sisters, Maria
and Elizabeth, lost their lives to galloping consumption, a condition most
certainly brought about by the poor conditions of the school environment.

The governess was considered a "respected" position, yet in most cases,
women were treated cruelly by their employers and looked down on by most
members of society. A passage in *Jane Eyre* illustrates what seemed to be the
general opinion of the real role of the governess in English society:

"No—you men never do consider economy and common
sense. You should hear mama on the chapter of governesses:
Mary and I have had, I should think, a dozen at least in our day;
half of them detestable and the rest ridiculous, and all incubi —
were they not, mama?"

"Did you speak, my own?"

The young lady thus claimed as the dowager's special property,
reiterated her question with an explanation.

"My dearest, don't mention governesses; the word makes me
nervous. I have suffered a martyrdom from their incompetency
and caprice; I thank Heaven I have now done with them" (179).

Such sentiments are echoed in *Shirley*, where a former governess cautions
against this as a choice for employment:

The gentleman I found regarded me as a tabooed woman, to
whom they were interdicted from granting the usual privileges of
the sex and yet who annoyed them by frequently crossing their
path. The ladies too made it plain that they thought me "a bore."
The servants, it was signified, "detested me" why I could never
comprehend. . .(281).

Even her charge, Shirley, scoffs at the position, stating, "What an idea! Be a governess! Better be a slave at once" (180).

Abuse from the employers was frequent, but often problems from the children made such positions even more unbearable: "The behavior of the children tended to reveal and reflect the attitude of their parents. There was sometimes respect and affection, but more often there was disobedience, snobbery, and sometimes physical cruelty."[15] What Agnes Grey faces from her young charges and their parents is horrifying. In the opening pages of the novel, young Tom Bloomfield tells Agnes that he likes to trap birds so he can "cut them into pieces with a penknife" or "roast them alive" just so see how long the creatures will live. He tells Agnes that she will see him hit his sister because "I'm obliged to do it now and then to keep her in order" (17). His sister's behavior is not much better. Lesson plans are interrupted when the child drops to the floor "like a leaden weight" and screams "loud, shrill, piercing screams" that bring her mother running to the scene (28). That ends in only Agnes being scolded by the parents, for "I had no rewards to offer, and as for punishments, I was given to understand, the parents reserved that privilege to themselves; and yet they expected me to keep my pupils in order" (24).

Whether their characters are placed in positions of governesses or teachers, social class plays an important part in Brontë novels. Terry Eagleton remarks that while the structure of Anne Brontë's novels is relatively simple compared with the works of Emily and Charlotte, the same idea is used in all the Brontë novels:

> . . .a pious heroine is flanked by a morally lax upper class on the one hand and a principled hero on the other; and each book ends with her extrication from the clutches of the first and her embracing of the alternative values offered by the second.[16]

These alternative values, while not always the most ideal, clearly offer a way out of the Brontës' burdensome situations.

POSTCOLONIAL INTERPRETATIONS

In the Victorian era, England not only faced many changes at home, but also took on the role as head of an empire. At the height of its power, England ruled over lands in the Caribbean, Australia, New Zealand, and Africa. Rudyard Kipling used the phrase "white man's burden" to mean the important responsibility that the British had in "civilizing" the native people of this empire. While some writers did explore the worlds of the empire (most specifically, E.M. Forester's *A Passage to India;* Joseph Conrad's *Heart of Darkness;* and Kipling's *Kim),* most of the time the images are carefully relegated to the background.

Postcolonial critics, when examining Victorian novels, explain that images of the colonized are often characterized by those who colonized them. In the mid-1980s, Gayatri Spivak turned critics' heads to the representation of those from the empire when she examined the role of Bertha, the "mad" West Indian wife of Rochester in *Jane Eyre.* Other critics have linked the appearance of Bertha as merely another part of Jane. Helene Moglen states that "Bertha has from the beginning functioned as a warning against the consequences of Jane's desire for emotional release," [17] and Sandra Gilbert and Susan Gubar see Bertha as Jane's "dark double throughout the governess's stay at Thornfield."[18] However, Spivak suggests that the character of Bertha Mason is produced "by the axiomatics of imperialism." [19] Certainly, through the eyes of Jane herself, Bertha is seen as little more than an animal:

> In the deep shade, at the further end of the room, a figure ran backwards and forwards. What it was, whether beast or human being, one could could not, at first sight, tell: it groveled, seemingly, on all fours; it snatched and growled like some strange, wild animal, but it was covered with clothing; and a quality of dark, grizzled hair, wild as a mane, hid its head and face (290).

The only real image of Bertha is thus created through the eyes of Jane and Rochester, who fail to regard her as a human being. Such "nonhuman" depictions of those from the lands of the British Empire are not unknown in the Victorian novel, and Susan Meyer suggests that fear may be a motivation for such images. This fear, according to Meyer, can be seen in both *Shirley,* where the main hero threatens to leave to take a North American savage as a wife, and *Villette,* where Lucy's lover departs to the West Indies, never to be seen again.[20] Surely such images suggest fear of the unknown people of the British Empire.

Critics have remarked that *Wuthering Heights* seems to be contrived in a world that is far away from the worries of Victorian industrialization and the British Empire, yet passages in the novel suggest that Heathcliff himself may have either been a product of that empire, or gained his wealth from the empire. Certainly, when he is introduced as a "gipsy brat," he is christened as an outsider even though the family named him Heathcliff after a son who died at birth. Although it is unclear where he gained his great wealth during his disappearance, the idea cannot be readily dismissed that he, like many people of the Victorian era, gained riches from property in the lands of the empire.

Although Anne seems to be engulfed with the worries of Victorian England at home, glimpses of colonization can also be seen in *Agnes Grey*, in which the young heroine compares the movement to her second post as a governess with being "dropped from the clouds into a remote and unknown land, widely and completely isolated from all she had ever seen or known before, like waking to find yourself in New Zealand" with a world of waters between (58). Apparently, this young governess viewed her surroundings as foreign, mysterious, and frightening, much like the English colonizers viewed the lands of the empire.

In 1965, the author Jean Rhys—who had been moved by the character of Bertha Mason—published her version of the story of Rochester's first wife as seen through Bertha's eyes. The novel, *Wide Sargasso Sea*, not only gave a voice to this "mad" character from the West Indies, but also encouraged closer interpretations of *Jane Eyre*. More recently, *Here on Earth*, by Alice Hoffman, tells the tale of a destructive love between two characters who closely resemble the tormented Heathcliff and Catherine. In film, the images of Jane Eyre and Rochester, as well as those of Catherine and Heathcliff, have haunted the screen in many productions. Probably the most famous is the 1939 version of *Wuthering Heights*, which starred the dark, mysterious Laurence Olivier and the exotically beautiful Merle Oberon.

The Brontë sisters made their mark on nineteenth-century British society, but their stories endure. Through film, art, and critical interpretations, their works continue to be examined and praised, and assured their rightful place in literary history.

NOTES

1. Elizabeth Langland, *Anne Brontë: The Other One* (London: Macmillan, 1989), 153.

2. Maggie Berg, *Jane Eyre: Portrait of a Life* (Boston: Twayne Publishers, 1987), 2.

3. Ellen Moers, *Literary Women* (New York: Doubleday, 1976), 126.

4. Diane Long Hoeveler, *Gothic Feminism: The Professionalization of Gender From Charlotte Smith to the Brontës* (University Park: The Pennsylvania State University Press, 1998), 189.

5. Ibid., 193.

6. Ibid., 191.

7. Ibid., 204.

8. Robert Heilman, "Charlotte Brontë's 'New Gothic,'" in *The Victorian Novel: Modern Essays in Criticism,* ed. Ian Watt (New York: Oxford University Press, 1971), 168.

9. Ibid., 169.

10. Ibid., 176.

11. Nicholas Marsh, *Emily Brontë: Wuthering Heights* (New York: St. Martin's Press, 1999), 196.

12. Bettina Knapp, *The Brontës: Branwell, Anne, Emily, Charlotte* (New York: Continuum Publishing Company, 1991), 98–99.

13. Patricia Beer, *Reader, I Married Him: A Study of the Women Characters of Jane Austen, Charlotte Brontë, Elizabeth Gaskell, and George Eliot.* (London: Macmillan, 1974), 92.

14. W.A. Craik, *The Bronte Novels* (London: Methuen Company, 1968), 231.

15. M. Jeanne Peterson, "The Victorian Governess," in *Suffer and Be Still: Women in the Victorian Age,* ed. Martha Vicinus (Bloomington: Indiana University Press, 1972), 12.

16. Terry Eagleton, *Myths of Power: A Marxist Study of the Brontës* (London: Macmillan, 1975), 122.

17. Helene Moglen, *Charlotte Brontë: The Self-Conceived,* (New York: W.W. Norton Company, 1976), 126.

18. Sandra Gilbert and Susan Gubar, *The Madwoman in the Attic: The Woman Writer and the Nineteenth-Century Literary Imagination* (New Haven: Yale University Press, 1979), 360.

19. Gayartri Chakravorty Spivak, "Three Women's Texts and a Critique of Imperialism," *Critical Inquiry* 12 (1985): 247.

20. Susan Meyer, "Colonism and the Figurative Strategy of *Jane Eyre,*" *Victorian Studies* 33.2 (1990): 247.

T. E. APTER

Romanticism and Romantic Love in Wuthering Heights

A Romantic conception of romantic love can easily wilt and stew in a sickening sweet decay. When it supposes itself to be poignantly in bloom it may be stifled by an escapist's self-massaging imagination. This is the fate of Goethe's Werther who luxuriates in his pain, crying his heart out among gnarled oaks until he shoots himself in the hope that he will eventually be united with his love in the world to come. This is also the fate of Goethe's Ottilie and Eduard in *Elective Affinities* who expire through unfulfillable love (Ottilie, like Heathcliff, starves herself to death) and join one another in the grave. Goethe saw both these loves as irrational passions which could not be satisfied within the moral world and the idea of unity in death was an attempt to reconcile the passion with morality. These attempts to portray romantic passion in the language of Romanticism fail to make either the tragedy or the love convincing. Inadvertently the passion is portrayed as a weak thing, nourished for the sake of anguished ornamentation. Pain is valued because it supposedly measures intense emotion, but because the emphasis is on the self-reflecting pain, the love has no real intensity. The inclination for torment and the idea that there is depth in pain mistake themselves for the substance of tragic love. *Wuthering Heights* is a study of romantic love undertaken by a Romantic imagination, but it contains a serious study of the destructive elements within the magnetism of anguish and passion alongside a potent expression of their value and projects a far more original and useful

From *The Art of Emily Brontë*, edited by Anne Smith. © 1976 by Vision Press. Reprinted by permission.

resolution of irrational passion and morality than death while nonetheless expressing sympathy with that old Romantic solution.

The elements in the Catherine/Heathcliff theme which place it clearly within a Romantic tradition include an involvement with nature so intense, so mystical that it contains a death wish, or, more specifically, a desire to return to the mindless unity of nature, to mend the separation from nature effected by society and sophistication; also included are a love which longs for a soul unity with the beloved, a love which grows viciously single-minded when thwarted, and circumstances which prohibit the earthly satisfaction of love. But it is part of Emily Brontë's complete lack of sentimentality that she shows the prohibitive circumstances to stem from the characters' own destructive and self-destructive impulses; for although every Romantic knows that passion involves suffering, he does not often admit that the characters who enjoy the intensity of passion also enjoy, and are willing to generate, the suffering from which the intensity issues, and that it is the impulse to destroy, or rather, the capacity to value something only in its absence, or through torturous trials, that gives rise to the Romantic tragedy of love. Usually the relishing of pain takes place in the artist's imagination, spinning tales of doom and destruction which innocent characters must then enact, but Emily Brontë carries this problem of the Romantic imagination into the tale itself, and thus the meaning of that typical suffering is given a new depth and a new criticism.

The emphasis in *Wuthering Heights* is on the reality of passion. The novel insists that passion is a force with its own laws, a cosmic, inhuman thing that cannot be denied or treated lightly, and if the people who have passion disregard it, they will be divided against themselves and destroyed by their defiance. But not everyone is subject to its laws, for not everyone is able to enter the sphere in which passion is a reality. The book opens with a mistaken conception of deep feeling and deep suffering. Lockwood supposes himself to be within the world of Romantic disappointment and isolation. At first he identifies Heathcliff as a fellow member of this clan. He is in fact correct to see Heathcliff as an intriguing Romantic figure, but this correctness is ironic because Lockwood's own conception of the Romantic cult is so mistaken. When Heathcliff shouts rudely at the lovely young Cathy, Lockwood supposes his initial impression of Heathcliff to be wrong because he now sees Heathcliff as a thoroughly hard, unsentimental man; but Lockwood is mistaken in thinking that a Romantically isolated, anguished figure must have essentially a kind heart, that isolation and anguish are only surface wounds covering a good, normal nature. In short, Lockwood makes the mistake that many would-be Romantic artists make; he supposes suffering on passion's account to be a good excuse for poignant ornamentation.

Again, Lockwood is right to see Heathcliff as a misanthrope, but he is ridiculous in supposing that he shares Heathcliff's attitudes, for he does not know what it means to be misanthropic. For Lockwood misanthropy is merely an attractive posture. There is real anger directed towards Lockwood by the author not merely because he is shallow but because he is shallow and considers himself to be deep. In this anger a jealousy of depth is felt: only those who truly suffer emotional intensity have a right to claim its glamour. Though Lockwood has an impulse to destroy love—he once fancied himself in love but grew cold when he saw that his attraction was returned, and he toys with the idea of winning young Cathy's love, but decides against it in case her temper should turn out to be as bad as her mother's—his self defeat comes from a source far inferior to the source of Catherine's or Heathcliff's destructive impulses. In Lockwood's case fear of emotion rather than emotional greed or bitter vengefulness leads him to believe he is a highly emotional person; because he tries to avoid emotional contact he assumes that his problem stems from the overwhelming intensity of his feelings; but there is no doubt in the author's mind that however horrendous Heathcliff's soul is, it is more significant than Lockwood's soul. This hierarchy of values underlines a Romantic pride in the strength of emotion, be the strength good or ill.

The good and ill, however, are not irrelevant. Early critics of the novel complained that the work was without moral design, but it is difficult to believe they actually meant that. There are numerous references to the devil and heaven and hell: Heathcliff is nearly as dark as if he came from the devil; he is prepared to defy the devil in order to protect Catherine from the Linton's dog; Hindley calls him an "imp of Satan"; in her diary the young Catherine writes that "Joseph asseverated 'owd Nick' would fetch us sure as we were living", and the sober Nelly also expresses her puzzlement as to what sort of creature Heathcliff is, implying that he might be some kind of demon. Although such references need not have a moral focus—they could be used simply for eerie effect, as in a ghost story—Emily Brontë uses them to emphasize the inhuman and demonic aspects of passion, and undoubtedly the early critics' real complaint lay not with a lack of moral design but with the particular moral design. The novel continually questions where in the human and extra-human world passion lies; and though its value is never undermined, passion is not seen to be a warm, tender thing, full of the goodness of life or neatly tied to compassionate, considerate feelings.

It is primarily the pontificating Joseph, self-righteously using religious vindictiveness as an excuse for his own sadism, and Hindley, who is afraid of his position vis-à-vis Heathcliff, who express belief in this goblin-like wickedness; but other characters, too, through fear and incomprehension, share this sense of a demon in Heathcliff. Isabella asks in her desperate letter to Nelly, written after her marriage, "What kind of man is he?" and in his last meeting with Catherine Nelly says "I did not feel as if I were in the company of a creature of my own species; it appeared that he would not understand, though I spoke to him; so I stood off, and held my tongue, in great perplexity" (XV, 134). Heathcliff, as the embodiment of relentlessly single-minded passion, does not even speak the same language as ordinary, sociable humans. People do not fear him simply because he is cruel, but because he is unbelievably cruel while following his own moral law—passion's law. As he is dying Nelly suggests he make his peace with God, but he replies that he has done nothing wrong, and Catherine, when she is dying, admits that he has done nothing wrong. The lovers are not concerned with humanity's law, they are concerned with passion's law, and this law is shown to be startlingly different from the laws in which Joseph and Hindley and Nelly and Lockwood believe. Ordinarily love is thought to redeem destructive impulses, but in Heathcliff's case it is his love for Catherine which motivates his cruelty. He would not have minded Hindley's degradation if Catherine had stood by him; but because that degradation led to Catherine's rejection, he must destroy Hindley. He would not have bothered with Edgar Linton and his family had Catherine not married Edgar. His revenge is of primary importance and must overcome his affection for Hareton; as Hindley's child Hareton must be the object of revenge. Indeed, Heathcliff's savagery is not without sentimentality, for it is thoroughly unredeemed, indulgently consistent, and this exaggeration puts it out of focus. The more interesting factor is the love which is its cause.

What kind of love demands such destruction? Though the love between Catherine and Heathcliff is seen as a terrible and valuable force, there is no divinity or even nobility in it, no embodiment of human ideals. It is a rigidly personal, specific connection, forged by habit, without illusion, without respect, but a connection so strong that it defies the notion of separation. The dying Catherine recalls how painful it was when, at the age of twelve, Hindley prevented her and Heathcliff from sharing the same bed. Their clothes, as children, are often mingled: Catherine fastens her and Heathcliff's pinafores together to form a curtain round them, and they want a woman's cloak—one cloak—to shelter them on a scamper across the moor. Unlike Goethe's novels of love and death there is no sense here that this love would not live up to expectation. In *Wuthering Heights* the union desired in death is not an easy assertion of a nice but not quite believable connection; the union in death is seen as a point towards which inexorable forces are moving. Catherine's speech about her love for Heathcliff resembling "the eternal rocks beneath—a source of little visible delight, but necessary" (IX, 74) has a ring of sentimentality, but the support it gets from the rest of the novel absorbs the false tone. Her language is self-indulgent, but she is fighting to understand the depth of her attachment to Heathcliff at the very moment she has tried, by promising to marry Edgar, to deny that attachment; she is not simply enjoying a Romantic pose.

Their attachment defines their world and provides their own morality. Together they can settle down comfortably to await the advent of "owd Nick" threatened by Joseph because the hell of others has no meaning to them as long as they are together. Furthermore, the heaven of others is rejected by Catherine; she dreams that she finds herself in heaven and weeps because she is separated from the Heights, and the angels, angry with her blasphemous dissatisfaction, throw her from heaven, and she awakes on the Heights, sobbing for joy. When Nelly advises Heathcliff to prepare for death he answers that he has nearly attained his heaven—and his heaven is death, and union with Catherine. No laws other than those which pertain to their attachment are binding upon them. When Isabella declares her love for Heathcliff, Catherine tells her that he is "a fierce, pitiless, wolfish man". She never says to him "let this or that enemy alone, because it would be ungenerous or cruel to harm them, I say—'Let them alone because *I* should hate them to be wronged'," (X, 90). And Heathcliff spurns the idea of Edgar looking after the altered, ailing Catherine on grounds of Christian charity and duty. To him such bonds are paltry things in contrast to the love which would bind him to her.

Their love, however, does go wrong; but even in the thwarting of their attachment only the laws of passion are relevant; they are not separated by an outside force—no outside force would be strong enough to eclipse their emotions. The crux of the tensions which both bind them together and tear them apart can be seen in the episode in which Catherine, having returned to the Heights after her first visit to the Lintons, is anxious to return her new friends' hospitality and quarrels with Heathcliff because he is too dirty to receive her guests. He sulks for a while, but then asks Nelly to make him look decent. She replies:

> 'High time, Heathcliff,' I said, 'you *have* grieved Catherine; she's sorry she ever came home, I dare say! It looks as if you envied her, because she is more thought of than you.'
>
> The notion of *envying* Catherine was incomprehensible to him, but the notion of grieving her he understood clearly enough.
>
> 'Did she say she was grieved?' he inquired, looking very serious.

'She cried when I told her you were off again this morning.'
'Well, *I* cried last night,' he returned, 'and I had more reason
to cry than she' (VII, 53).

The incomprehensibility of envy comes from a complete identification of
interests, and is combined with a fierce protectiveness of the other's interests.
When Heathcliff watches Catherine through the window of Thrushcross
Grange as the Lintons, having thrown him out, comb Catherine's hair and
wash her wounded foot, his purpose is to determine whether she wants to be
rescued. If she does, then he will smash the window to save her; but when he
sees that she is content, he leaves. The reader is clearly aware of his
loneliness, but Heathcliff does not sulk over his exclusion. He waited by the
window, not to savour his unhappiness, but simply to determine whether
Catherine needed him.

This lack of envy is tied to his lack of common jealousy. When Edgar
becomes Catherine's husband Heathcliff refrains from killing him because he
is afraid that Catherine would suffer from this loss, and he claims that he
would never banish Edgar from her society as long as she desired his. But the
staunch protectiveness and identification of interests implied in his inability
to understand the notion of envying Catherine, is cancelled by the full
meaning of "but the notion of grieving her he understood clearly enough".
Nelly is remarkably insensitive to Heathcliff's attitude when she says to him,
"if you be ashamed of your touchiness, you must ask pardon, mind, when she
comes in", for his concern about her grief is not a straightforward concern
lest she be grieved. The notion of grieving her is important to him because
through the extent of her grief he can measure her attachment to him and by
grieving her he can remind her of that attachment when she tries to deny it.
"Well, *I* cried last night, and I had more reason to cry than she",—this is not
a simple childish competition; it is a means of punishment and reassurance,
pride's refuge when their union seems threatened. How can he sympathize
with her pain when her pain stems from her attempt to deny him? And, in
turn, Catherine is angry with him because his grief at her insults hurts her,
and it is wrong for him to hurt her. Sometimes the spiral is controlled.
Sometimes others wound Heathcliff more than Catherine has done, and so
it is not out of place for her to comfort him; she does not have to admit
herself in the wrong to do so. But the tension of their grieving one another
is explosive when it survives the comparative safety of childhood behaviour.
Here is Catherine at her last earthly meeting with Heathcliff:

'. . . and should a word of mine distress you hereafter, think I feel
the same distress underground, and for my own sake, forgive me!

... Nay, if you nurse anger, that will be worse to remember than my harsh words!

... Oh, you see, Nelly! he would not relent a moment, to keep me out of the grave! *That* is how I am loved!' (XV, 133–4).

Heathcliff's anger will be worse to remember than her harsh words, but it was caused by her harsh words and she would have been furious if Heathcliff did not get angry with her (as she is furious with her husband when he does not get angry with her). She taunts Heathcliff with the image of himself visiting her grave with wife and children by his side, whom he will love more than he now loves her, and he groans at this picture, he feels how strongly it denies his love for her; yet still she is not satisfied with his love; nor is there any way he could satisfy her emotional greed.

Their naturally forged union has been broken by Catherine's marriage and now they must struggle for possession of one another. This struggle is a desperate attack; they cannot be gentle with one another; they must be ruthless in their attempt to maintain their hold upon one another:

'I wish I could hold you,' she continued, bitterly, ''till we were both dead! I shouldn't care what you suffered. I care nothing for your sufferings. Why shouldn't you suffer? I do! Will you forget me—will you be happy when I am in the earth? ...'

'Don't torture me till I'm as mad as yourself,' cried he, wrenching his head free, and grinding his teeth.

... Her present countenance had a wild vindictiveness in its white cheek, and a bloodless lip, and scintillating eye; and she retained in her closed fingers, a portion of the locks she had been grasping. As to her companion, while raising himself with one hand, he had taken her arm with the other; and so inadequate was his stock of gentleness to the requirements of her condition, that on his letting go, I saw four distinct impressions left blue in the colourless skin (XV, 133).

Catherine's assertion that she cares nothing for Heathcliff's sufferings does not mean that she is actually indifferent to them. She wants him to suffer; only through his suffering will she be assured of his love for her after she is dead. The "wild vindictiveness" she expresses here is not the hatred and revulsion seen in the love and death struggle between Gudrun and Gerald in *Women in Love*; it is important that Heathcliff's and Catherine's love is not ambivalent as the possessive loves Lawrence portrays; this love becomes a lurid struggle for possession because its intensity and singleness, i.e., its lack of ambivalence, has been ignored by Catherine. But their anger towards one another is never hatred, and the physical pain they inflict upon one another at this meeting is a straightforward expression of love.

This vicious struggle for possession undermines Catherine's assertion that she *is* Heathcliff; but, because she believes this herself, she thinks it safe for her to marry Edgar Linton: Heathcliff is within her soul, therefore nothing can dislodge him. Nonetheless, it is clear from the way they wound one another that each is in continual need of reassurance—something that occurs only between two separate people. Catherine thinks only of her reassurance of her own feelings. She does not consider Heathcliff's need for proof of those feelings. She does not believe she needs to behave in accordance with her feelings, and so, blind to the meaning of her action, she marries Edgar. Heathcliff demands of her:

> '*Why* did you betray your own heart, Cathy? I have not one word of comfort. You deserve this. You have killed yourself . . . You loved me—then what *right* had you to leave me? . . . Because misery, and degradation, and death, and nothing that God or Satan could inflict would have parted us, you, of your own will, did it. I have not broken your heart—you have broken it—and in breaking it, you have broken mine.' (XV, 134–5).

"What *right* had you to leave me?" is the cry of outraged passion. Catherine thought she could slip beneath passion's net and take the offer of Edgar's pleasant love, but she is destroyed by her defiance. Her own emotional greed is drawn like a noose round Heathcliff's neck, but she thought he would be satisfied by her own inward assurance that they were one person. Her passion was so real that marriage to her had no reality.

The success of the Catherine/Heathcliff theme depends upon the felt potency of their love, and Mrs Leavis in her classic essay on *Wuthering Heights* complains that Emily Brontë does not show their shared interests, and wonders what they conversed about during their adult companionship;[1] but it is difficult to believe that such knowledge is actually necessary to understanding their attachment. Their shared interests are one another and one another's company. They fought and played and walked much as they had done as children. But it is true that the development and continuation of their attachment is taken for granted. The strength of their attachment is expressed not in dramatic episodes but in extremely effective Romantic rhetoric. The author achieves this rare success partly through oblique presentation of the lovers' outbursts; thus, a direct request for sympathy never embarrasses the reader. Heathcliff's first Tristanesque cry is presented through Lockwood's eyes, and at first the emphasis seems to be on the horror of Heathcliff's fascination with the spectre Lockwood has seen in a dream and which has so terrified him that the apparently ordinary man behaves towards the spectral waif with vicious cruelty. The keen sympathy then forced from the reader comes as a surprise:

> 'Come in! come in!' he sobbed. 'Cathy, do come. Oh, *do*— *once* more! Oh, my heart's darling, hear me *this* time—Catherine, at last!' (III, 33).

This cry is heard only once in the novel, yet it carries the force of a relentless repetition. "Hear me *this* time," shows how many times Heathcliff has called to her. Even before the story is known (for at this point Lockwood is ignorant of his landlord's history) the hopeless longing and deadly despair are clear. And when, in Werther fashion, Heathcliff beats his head upon the knotted oak in rage and grief at Catherine's death, sentimentality is just about overcome by Nelly's response: "It hardly moved my compassion—it appalled me". The Romantic exaggeration is effective because its point is not to pull heart strings but to lay bare the inexorable strength of grief and passion.

Catherine's outbursts, on the other hand, do not belong to the Romantic tradition of *Angst*. Always her emotional fits are fits of temper and are undercut by Nelly's impatience. Of Catherine as a child Nelly says, "She beat Hareton, or any child at a good fit of passionate crying". (Imagine an old nurse of Werther's saying "He always did go on a bit much about things". In Goethe's novel passionate fits are valued for their own sake; they are signs of emotional intensity and therefore are good. It is part of the effective Romanticism in *Wuthering Heights* that intensity is seen as a harsh necessity for some natures, not as a decorative thing, and when intensity is indulgently cultivated, it is shown to be so.) And as an adult, angry with Edgar's insistence that she see no more of Heathcliff, Catherine is no more, Nelly says, than a wailing, spoiled child who works herself up to the point of illness. Indeed, Catherine's despair stems from having broken with her childhood; her childish wailing expresses a longing to return to the time when she was able to be at one with her passion. Her illness and frustration stem from the inability to absorb the deepest part of herself within her adult life:

> 'But, supposing at twelve years old, I had been wrenched from the Heights, and every early association, and my all in all, as Heathcliff was at that time, and been converted at a stroke into Mrs Linton, the lady of Thrushcross Grange, and the wife of a stranger; an exile and outcast, thenceforth, from what had been my world—' (XII, 107).

This fantasy evokes impatience rather than compassion, for Catherine herself is responsible for this harsh transformation; *she* has wrenched herself from the Heights and from Heathcliff. Nonetheless her longing and frustration have an hypnotic pathos:

> 'Oh, I'm burning! I wish I were out of doors—I wish I were a girl again, half savage, and hardy, and free; and laughing at injuries, not maddening under them!' (XII, 107).

The hot, closed room at Thrushcross Grange becomes a prison. Repeatedly she begs Nelly to open a window. Her sense of being stifled by illness and emotional conflict, her vision of the Heights as she leans out of the window, set her within a world impossibly out of contact with the world in which she must live. Her longing rips up reality and fires her dreams with a deathly life; but Catherine's escapism is not the author's, and though the longing is startlingly vivid, there is no suggestion that the author shares it.

Though Emily Brontë does not straightforwardly endorse a scheme of value based upon emotional intensity alone, Catherine and Heathcliff do. When Edgar, as Catherine's husband, wants to know whether she will continue her friendship with Heathcliff even after he has eloped with Isabella and threatened violence to himself, she dismisses his morality of family loyalty and asserts her own:

> 'Oh, for mercy's sake,' interrupted the mistress, stamping her foot, 'for mercy's sake, let us hear no more of it now! Your cold blood cannot be worked into a fever; your veins are full of ice-water, but mine are boiling, and the sight of such chillness makes them dance' (XI, 101).

Edgar's arguments have no point because they are not expressed with passion. Her argument against him is simply that she is passionate. Heathcliff, too, continually asserts his rights on the grounds that his feelings are the stronger. He insists, when Edgar banishes him from Catherine's company, that his own emotions are finer:

> 'and there you see the distinction between our feelings. Had he been in my place, and I in his, though I hated him with a hatred that turned my life to gall, I never would have raised a hand against him. You may look incredulous, if you please! I never would have banished him from her society, as long as she desired his' (XIV, 125).

He despises Edgar for the character of his concern for Catherine and believes that the lower grade of her husband's feelings gives him the right to claim her:

> 'But do you imagine that I shall leave Catherine to his *duty* and *humanity*? and can you compare my feelings respecting Catherine, to his?' (XIV, 125).

Isabella, too, tries to play their Romantic game. When Catherine is incredulous at her declaration of love for Heathcliff, she replies, "I love him more than you ever loved Edgar". But Isabella does not really understand this Romantic universe. Like Lockwood, she merely fancies herself to be among the passionate ones. Like Lockwood, she believes that suffering for the sake of one's emotions is an attractive, glamorous thing. Her misunderstanding of passion's and cruelty's reality, destroys her.

In ordinary terms Catherine and Heathcliff are unfair in their assessment of Edgar's feelings, for he certainly does love Catherine; but at no time do his feelings rise to the Romantic standard. After Catherine's death Nelly says of him:

> 'But he was too good to be thoroughly unhappy long. *He* didn't pray for Catherine's soul to haunt him. Time brought resignation, and a melancholy sweeter than common joy. He recalled her memory with ardent, tender love, and hopeful aspiring to the better world, where, he doubted not, she was gone' (XVII, 151).

How Catherine would have despised his *resignation* and *hopeful aspiring* and *melancholy sweeter than common joy*. She has, after all, said, "If I were only sure it would kill him, . . . I'd kill myself directly!" (XII, 104). From her point of view Edgar's return to life would be a betrayal. She would feel that Edgar had no right to live because she had suffered and died. Even Heathcliff, who gives her everything, has difficulty in giving her enough. While she is dying she taunts Heathcliff with his strength and asks how many years he intends to live after she is dead. He demands of her:

> 'Is it not sufficient for your infernal selfishness, that while you are at peace I shall writhe in the torments of hell?'
> 'I shall not be at peace,' moaned Catherine. . . . (XV, 133).

Catherine believes that others should die because she has to die, and she accuses both Edgar and Heathcliff of killing her; but once she has passed childhood, and her inability to integrate her emotions into her behaviour shows its poisoning effects, she actually longs for her own death. The desire to return to childhood, the wish for regression and stagnation, is a wish for death, and in her adult life this death wish becomes integrally connected with her love for Heathcliff:

> 'And,' added she, musingly, 'the thing that irks me most is this shattered prison, after all. I'm tired, tired of being enclosed here. I'm wearying to escape into that glorious world, and to be always there; not seeing it dimly through tears, and yearning for it through the walls of an aching heart; but really with it, and in it' (XV, 134).

She is proud of this wish to escape into death, into the glorious world of her imagination. She believes herself to be better than other people because she desires this, and because the desire will soon be fulfilled:

> 'Nelly, you think you are better and more fortunate than I, in full health and strength. You are sorry for me—very soon that will be altered. I shall be sorry for *you*. I shall be incomparably beyond and above you all' (XV, 134).

Her death is the means by which she can satisfy her love for Heathcliff—and it is not even the adult Heathcliff she loves, for the real Heathcliff can be so tormented by her emotional greed and accusations that he turns lividly away from her. When the real Heathcliff hurts her because she sees how much she has hurt him, she says, "Never mind, that is not my Heathcliff. I shall have mine yet". Her love is not a longing for anything in this world; it is a longing for an impossible freedom from emotional conflict and her own excessive demands. Heathcliff shares her desire for death, but he does not want to die simply to regain a lost glorious world; he wants to die because Catherine is dying; he wants to join her in death. "Do I want to live?" he demands of her. "What kind of living will it be when you—oh, God! would *you* like to live with your soul in the grave?" (XV, 135). Catherine does not give a straightforward answer. "Let me alone, let me alone", she sobs; for the perplexing truth is that she does want to live with her soul in the grave. With her soul in the grave she will not be encumbered by her own nature; she will be free to identify with passion alone. In death she feels that the best and deepest part of herself will come alive.

Though Catherine can in part be blamed for the thwarted love between herself and Heathcliff, there is here, as in all cases of Romantic longing, a sense of the impossibility of fulfilment *no matter what*. The intensity of the desire involves an excitement which is far from the pleasure and contentment implied in *happiness*. When Heathcliff returns after his long mysterious absence,

> Catherine flew upstairs, breathless and wild, too excited to show gladness; indeed, by her face, you would rather have surmised an awful calamity (X, 83).

The excited joy has to battle to find a place in reality; it seems impossible to sustain it in the ordinary world. Catherine "kept her gaze fixed on him as if she feared he would vanish were she to remove it" (X, 84). The inability to trust the reality stems from a nervous intensity which is never resolved. The satisfaction of her longing would be explosive, annihilating. Only death is deep and dark enough to absorb the shock of fulfilment and bring the continuing peace which must follow that fulfilment.

Towards the end of his life Heathcliff becomes a Tristanesque figure, longing for the union with Catherine which will be his death. When he feels close to the realization of his desire he calls himself happy, but it is clear that he is tormented by a mingling of excitement and pain. The young Cathy describes to Hareton how he appeared:

> 'Why almost bright and cheerful—No, almost nothing—*very much* excited, and wild and glad!' (XXIV, 257).

While Heathcliff stands at the open window, watching for Catherine, he is pale, he trembles, there is a "strange joyful glitter in his eyes", and he breathes "as fast as a cat". The description is of one possessed, demonic, but not of someone who is *happy*. The anticipation is unbearable, and he must struggle towards death. He says to Nelly:

> '. . . you might as well bid a man struggling in the water, rest within arms-length of the shore! I must reach it first, and then I'll rest . . . I'm too happy, and yet I'm not happy enough. My soul's bliss kills my body, but does not satisfy itself' (XXXIV, 262).

The metaphor is ironic, for Heathcliff is swimming towards death, not to a life-sustaining shore; but the irony underlines an essential element of Romanticism—the notion of death as a freer, finer form of life, the notion that death alone can sustain the exultation whose intensity and continuation are thwarted and deflected in life. Death provides for that impossible

Romantic combination: ecstasy and peace. Heathcliff's longing has grown to such a pitch that only in death can he rest. His longing makes life an impossible torment. The world, without Catherine, has become a hell: her ghost fills all material objects with her image, other people mock him with their resemblance to her, the entire world is "a dreadful collection of memoranda that she did exist, and that I have lost her!" (XXXIII, 255). Soon his "one universal idea" of joining himself with her in death triumphs; the anticipation carries a bliss of soul which kills his body; only in death is there satisfaction for this devouring Romantic passion.

The destructive, unsatisfiable, death-ridden elements of Romantic love are harshly underlined. There is no sweet nostalgic sense that the lovers might have been happy if only the world had been a bit kinder to them. This love, generated within a Romantic vision, is suffering love. But the harsh facts of such love are not related with a simple moralising tongue, and the main power of the novel does lie in the magnetism of Catherine's and Heathcliff's bond. However, Emily Brontë effectively and convincingly portrays an alternative to that destructive, Romantic love, keeping much of the vitality of the first love, but transforming it into something which can survive in this life.

Young Cathy Linton's nature is similar to that of her mother: she is lively, agile (she delights in swinging from tree branches twenty feet from the ground), pert, affectionate but not always gentle (she awakens Nelly by pulling her hair), proud of her strong emotions and healthy spirits; but the important difference between Cathy and her mother is Cathy's ability to care about hurting people in the sense of not wanting to hurt them, and her ability to suffer at the hands of others without feeling the need for revenge. When her father is ill she promises Nelly that she will not vex him:

> 'I love him better than myself, Ellen; and I know it by this: I pray every night that I may live after him, because I would rather be miserable than that he should be—that proves I love him better than myself' (XXII, 187).

This shows a complete reversal of her mother's feelings, for Catherine felt that others should suffer at the very least as much as herself. When young Cathy does cause a friend pain she is able to sustain a true regret. In her anger with Linton Heathcliff for insisting that her mother hated her father, she pushes his chair, and he is seized by a suffocating cough. Nelly says that Cathy then "wept with all her might, aghast at the mischief she had done" (XXIII, 192). Nor does she subsequently, as Catherine would have done, grow angry with Linton for upsetting her with the pain she has caused him.

Her mother's proud spirit is apparent, but without the vindictiveness:

> 'I'm sorry I hurt you Linton!' she said at length, racked beyond endurance. 'But *I* couldn't have been hurt by that little push; and I had no idea that you could, either—you're not much, are you, Linton? Don't let me go home thinking I've done you harm! answer, speak to me' (XXIII, 193).

Even when faced with Linton's reply, which is a pathetic version of Catherine's morality ("you've hurt me so, that I shall lie awake all night, choking with this cough! . . . but *you'll* be comfortably asleep, while I'm in agony") she presses forward kindly and regretfully, though she fully understands his game:

> 'He's good and patient, now. He's beginning to think I shall have far greater misery than he will to-night, if I believe he is the worse for my visit' (XXIII, 194).

Only when she is treated with sustained cruelty, when she is separated from those who love her and is tormented by the thought that they are worrying about her, does she become cold, aloof, unhelpful. However, even during her captivity at the Heights, her hostility towards her companions does not completely separate her from them. Nelly says that she complained of loneliness and "preferred quarrelling with Joseph in the kitchen to sitting at peace in her solitude" (XXII, 245). Cathy can work out her hostility through quarrelling whereas her mother could only work herself up. Cathy is able to notice what is happening to other people as she quarrels with them whereas Catherine's mind was devoured by rage and she could only see that people were hurting her. When Hareton is confined to the house on account of an arm injury Catherine is able to understand his pain at their mutual insults and they become friends. Her belief that people should be nice to her because it will make her happy, that they should forgive her unkindnesses because she demands it of them, has more warmth and playfulness, less "infernal selfishness" than similar demands made by her mother. Cathy is able to show gratitude rather than righteousness in the face of forgiveness; she is also able to be patient, and to forgive before forgiveness is granted her:

> 'Say you forgive me, Hareton, do! You can make me so happy, by speaking that little word.'
> He muttered something inaudible.
> 'And you'll be my friend?' added Catherine, interrogatively.

'Nay! You'll be ashamed of me every day of your life . . .'
'So, you won't be my friend?' she said, smiling as sweet as
honey, and creeping close up (XXXII, 248–9).

The love between Cathy and Hareton, like that between Catherine and
Heathcliff, is forged by habit, without illusion, without ideal. It is also nearly
incestuous—they are actually cousins, and Nelly says that they were both
really her children—but the close attachment will not confuse and destroy
them as it did Catherine and Heathcliff. The strength of their feelings can be
expressed in a playfulness which is connected to childhood play but is not
simply childish. Catherine and Heathcliff destroyed the possibility of
continuing such natural and easy expression of their love, and so the strength
of their emotion turned into a Romantic death-ridden passion. It was not
simply intense feeling which issued in this darkness; it was intense feeling
which demanded to be measured in suffering, and Emily Brontë's diagnosis
thus denies the debilitating aspect of the conventional Romantic picture, i.e.
that intense feeling cannot survive in this world. For it is only a certain way
of measuring emotion, not emotion itself, which explodes into death; it is
only a certain way of demanding proof of intense attachment, not the
attachment itself, which is destructive. Emily Brontë's assertion of the full-
blooded reality and possible survival of emotion gives strength both to the
Romantic tragedy of Catherine and Heathcliff and to the happiness of Cathy
and Hareton; neither the former couple's suffering nor the latter couple's
fulfilment is undercut by a conventionally benign Romanticism. Having
shown the harshness and potency of Romantic passion, Brontë concludes by
portraying a love which knows its measure without reference to tension and
pain.

NOTE

1. F. R. Leavis and Q. D. Leavis, *Lectures in America* (1969), p. 96.

W. A. CRAIK

Agnes Grey

No one could call Anne Brontë's two novels masterpieces; but she deserves neither to be ignored, nor to be regarded only as a pale copy of her sisters. She is absorbing on at least three, though not equal, counts: as the first novel writer of the family, using material later used by Emily and Charlotte; as a norm from which to judge the powers of her sisters in using such material; and as a novelist in her own right with a mode and flavour of her own— worthy of attention, original and good. She resembles Charlotte in having similar experiences to draw upon, and in feeling in her second novel a moral duty to write of an uncongenial topic; she resembles both her sisters in finding man's inhumanity to man a fitting element in a love story; and in being startlingly unconventional, unsophisticated, and candid. She uses some of the methods of both in organizing her material. But her own personality, her way of considering the experiences she puts before her heroines, and the idiom in which her heroines present them, are not so much akin to her sisters as to the eighteenth century. If the reader goes to Anne Brontë for what either Charlotte or Emily offers, he is disappointed. If he takes pleasure in Fanny Burney or Maria Edgeworth—or, to name a greater, Jane Austen—he will find her manner congenial and her writing attractive. While I propose to relate her novels to those of Charlotte or Emily where the connection is useful to either sister, I intend also to assess them on their own terms, for what they attempt and achieve.

From *The Brontë Novels* by W. A. Craik. (London: Methuen Company, 1969): pp.202–227. Reprinted by permission of Taylor and Francis.

Anne Brontë; has suffered like her sisters from the Brontë legend. She has also suffered from the sisters themselves. One thing that is best forgotten is the image of the 'gentle Anne', as she is termed by Charlotte and Arthur Nicholls, since without the legend and the comment one would not see much 'gentleness' in her, even in *Agnes Grey*. One thing well remembered however is that *Agnes Grey* is probably the first prose for publication written at Haworth Parsonage, and would be read and absorbed by her sisters before *Wuthering Heights*, *The Professor*, and the story it most resembles, *Jane Eyre*, were written. If any credit for conception is to be claimed it must be by Anne. The attempt must therefore be made to think of her with a mind reasonably uncoloured by *Jane Eyre* and *Wuthering Heights*, while not yet forgetting the juvenile fantasies that themselves colour all three.

Agnes Grey is an unpretentious work about an unpretentious heroine. It is probably a recasting of the work mentioned in the 'Birthday Note' of 1845, where she remarks: 'I have begun the third volume of *Passages in the life of an Individual*': a title more apt to what is now *Agnes Grey* than the one it possesses, which, like the story, is unassuming, and does not adequately suggest what is actually offered. One would summarize the main story as one in which a clergyman's younger daughter, compelled by her father's fallen fortunes to earn her living as a governess in two middle-class country families, and later, at his death, to help her mother run a small school, meets, while in her second place of employment, a worthy young clergyman whom she later marries. The other plot concerns the young and beautiful pupil, a coquette, who marries a degenerate young landowner for his money and position. Few plots could be less sensational; even *The Professor*, by contrast, seems a heady brew. Of the few exciting moments Anne Brontë; offers herself, she makes very little, reducing them by covering them briefly—as Agnes' father's death, which is comprised in a few words at the end of Chapter 18—or by a calm literal manner of telling—like her meeting with Mr Weston on the sands (Chapter 24) —or by a dash of astringent or sardonic humour—as when she suppresses her reply to Mrs Bloomfield:

'You seem to have forgotten,' said she calmly, 'that the creatures were all created for our convenience.'
I thought that the doctrine admitted some doubt.
(Chapter 5)

Clearly her aim is not excitement or sensation, and, as will later be examined, is not indicated properly by such a summary, which is actually misleading. One does not, in fact, read *Agnes Grey* for the story, and its importance does not lie in the story, a matter which immediately sets Anne Brontë apart from her sisters. Like Jane Austen, Anne Brontë, working her way through it without excitement or sensationalism, produces some unique incident, pungent characters, and, above all, a serious, penetrating and new exposure of society.

Also like Jane Austen, she keeps to what she knows. The material is plainly drawn from her own life. Anne Brontë herself is a clergyman's daughter, the youngest of the family, compelled to teach to earn her living, employed in the families of the gentry, while Agnes Grey's eventual modest though happy marriage is what Anne Brontë could without impropriety envisage for herself. Like Charlotte, she draws on more than herself. The loathsome Bloomfield children in her first post are the Inghams of Anne's first post at Blake Hall; the Murray household resembles closely that of the Robinsons, with whom she stayed some years, as Agnes stays with the Murrays.[1] Some of the most telling incident also is from life, notably the one that most readers remember best, in which Agnes destroys the nest of young birds to prevent a brutal child from torturing them.

It is as tempting therefore with Anne Brontë as with Charlotte to identify the narrator with the author, to consider that what is revealed of Agnes must also be true of Anne. It is not necessarily any more true of Agnes Grey than of Jane Eyre. While the narrative stance adopted in *Agnes Grey* is very much more simple than that of *Jane Eyre*, it is no mere autobiographical fantasy. Considerable degrees of detachment may be seen between the 'I' at different points in the narrative, and the 'I' who comments on them. Quite clearly the childish eighteen-year-old girl of the opening chapters is greatly below the narrator and also the reader, not only in quietly accepting that she is fit only to 'go and practise [her] music, or play with the kitten' (Chapter I), but in thinking that

> the clear remembrance of my own thoughts in early childhood would [in training children] be a surer guide than the instructions of the most mature adviser.
>
> (Chapter I)

As Agnes grows up the gap narrows, as it does as Jane Eyre grows up. But it never closes. Quite clearly the Agnes of the closing section is not only older but wiser than the young self narrating the events; yet at twenty-three, she still asks her mother's permission before accepting Mr Weston's invitation to a walk (Chapter 25). There is no suggestion, despite the moral and instructive tone of parts of the narrative, that this is the proper, or accepted, way to act for a woman of twenty-three (only a year younger than Lucy Snowe), as there is for instance in the works of Charlotte M. Yonge. Anne

Brontë always represents Agnes as someone younger and less experienced than herself or the reader, who is much less often on terms of wholehearted sympathy with her than with Jane Eyre. As a narrator, she has more in common with Esther Summerson in *Bleak House*.

She has in common with Esther that she also is not the absolute centre of interest. She is what makes the action cohere, but she is not necessarily the protagonist. She is the means by which the novel progresses, the author's purpose in it is achieved, and the events and characters are connected. But unlike *Jane Eyre's*, the important events concern others, notably Rosalie Murray, as much as herself, and the personalities she delineates are almost as clearly seen, and as interesting, as her own. One remembers Rosalie's flirtation with the rector Mr Hatfield better than Agnes's meetings with the curate Mr Weston, remembers the Bloomfield children's revolting habits more than the horror they inspire in Agnes; one sees the horse-loving Matilda or her mother 'who required neither rouge nor padding to add to her charms' (Chapter 7) quite as clearly as the quiet, plain, little heroine. Anne Brontë, while clearly showing, and expecting to elicit, sympathy for the hard-pressed Agnes, is not primarily concerned with her responses. Agnes does not actually create the reader's reaction to those with whom she comes into contact, nor do Anne Brontë and the reader judge them by how they treat her, as one judges those who come into contact with Jane Eyre. The whole of Rosalie's flirtation with Mr Hatfield proceeds without Agnes being moved by it at all, except to detached moral disapproval. Yet it is fully as significant and absorbing as Rosalie's next attempt, to flirt with Mr Weston, from which Agnes suffers considerable pain. What makes the second flirtation a graver matter than the first is what it reveals about Rosalie, that she is so taken up with coquetterie that she must descend from the willing and socially acceptable vicar to the unmoved and socially impossible curate. Agnes's feelings have very little to do with the artistic purpose here.

Agnes indeed as a personality can be effaced for quite long stretches. There are several points at which a secondary narrator supersedes her: as in Chapter II, where the cottager Nancy retails the contrasting visits and behaviour to her of the two clergymen, or in Chapter 14, where Rosalie tells her own story. These, and scenes in which the story is told to Agnes, who merely comments, bear a resemblance to the method of *Wuthering Heights*. There are also many points at which the scene proceeds by way of dialogue in which Agnes takes no part and passes no comment. If so neutral a narrator has a precedent, it is found in Scott's *Redgauntlet*, which opens with the letters to and fro of Alan Fairford and his friend Darsie Latimer, the bulk of the narrative being that of Fairford, who is no more the all-absorbing hero than is Agnes. Scott has soon to abandon the method; Anne Brontë can continue in it. It is clear that her purpose in using her material, and adopting the first-person narrator, is an original and largely self-taught one; it is not a tentative movement towards either Charlotte Brontë's or Emily's. She is attempting an examination of a section of society, which, seen from the unusual view that a governess enjoys, exposes itself, its standards, its follies, and its failings for the reader's assessment, not necessarily so that an unusual judgement may be passed, but so that long-held opinions may be rescrutinized, refreshed, and confirmed.

Such a purpose affects the relationship between author, narrator and reader. Anne Brontë never forgets either herself, her creation, or her reader. Identification with Agnes is impossible, because of the childishness already noted, nor can one ever lose oneself in the action, since it is usually either comic or reprehensible. Emotional response is called up for a purpose, so that understanding and appreciation shall, as with Jane Austen, lead to moral judgement, the way to which is pointed by a whole variety of means, all befitting Agnes, but all making the detachment between herself and the reader very clear. Anne Brontë assumes a reader as rational and reasonable as Agnes's most mature self. Sometimes her tone is of serious straightforward utterance of dicta known to both, and given because they summarize what has gone, or prepare what is to follow:

> Habitual associates are known to exercise a great influence over each other's minds and manners. Those whose actions are for ever before our eyes, whose words are ever in our ears, will naturally lead us, albeit, against our will—slowly—gradually—imperceptibly, perhaps, to act and speak as they do.
>
> (Chapter II)

It is with such well-grounded fears of her own deterioration in bad company that Agnes welcomes Mr Weston. Frequently she is much more oblique, as in her closing reply to Rosalie's wish

> 'to enjoy myself thoroughly, and coquet with all the world, till I am on the verge of being called an old maid; and then, to escape the infamy of that, after having made ten thousand conquests, to break all their hearts save one, by marrying some high-born, rich, indulgent husband, whom, on the other hand, fifty ladies were dying to have.'
>
> 'Well, as long as you entertain these views, keep single by all means, and never marry at all, not even to escape the infamy of old-maidenhood.'
>
> (Chapter 9)

The story begins

> All true histories contain instruction; though, in some, the
> treasure may be hard to find, and, when found, so trivial in
> quantity that the dry, shrivelled kernel scarcely compensates for
> the trouble of cracking the nut. Whether this be the case with my
> history or not, I am hardly competent to judge; I sometimes
> think it might prove useful to some, and entertaining to others,
> but the world may judge for itself: shielded by my own obscurity,
> and by the lapse of years, and a few fictitious names, I do not fear
> to venture, and will candidly lay before the public what I would
> not disclose to the most intimate friend.
>
> (Chapter I)

It never loses sight of its opening. The purpose revealed—to establish moral
standards, whether those of Agnes or others, to measure their conduct
against them, and thus establish the worth of both the conduct and of the
standards on which it is based—is plainly Anne Brontë's own, not her
character's, since Agnes modestly disclaims what her whole history is
designed to reveal—the possession of the 'treasure' of instruction. Agnes is
plainly rather a mask behind which her author may retire, than a means by
which, in Agnes's words, Anne Brontë herself can 'candidly lay before the
public what I would not disclose to the most intimate friend'. She is showing
herself ironically and wittily aware of the illusions of the fictional memoir
which involves so improbable a laying before the public, and so establishes
the terms on which she uses it. Anne Brontë, intending to be moral, avoids,
again like Jane Austen, ever alienating her reader by instructing him in
person. Agnes is her mouthpiece, a creation whose judgement the reader can
always trust, but who is yet sufficiently his inferior in years and experience to
make an appealing guide. The form of the candid, unsophisticated,
unprofessional memoir is one very suited both to such a purpose and such a
narrator. It makes the direct addresses to the reader acceptable and even
desirable. They are frequent:

> As I cannot, like Dogberry, find it in my heart to bestow *all* my
> tediousness on the reader, I will not go on to bore him with a
> minute detail of all the discoveries and proceedings of this and
> the following day.
>
> (Chapter 7)

A few more observations about Horton Lodge and its on goings, and I have done with dry description for the present.

(Chapter 7)

As I am in the way of confessions, I may as well acknowledge that, about this time, I paid more attention to dress than ever I had done before.

(Chapter 17)

The diffidence that provokes these remarks makes Agnes an engaging guide, and prevents her from being a pontifical or priggish one. While one may suspect that the author also is diffident, she is proved to have chosen her form well, since it turns what could have been a defect to good use.

The narrative method and the form are, indeed, more cunning than they seem. The story is basically in two main sections, one comprising Agnes's experiences with the appalling Bloomfield family at Wellwood (Chapters 2–5), the other her several years' stay with the Murrays at Horton Lodge (Chapters 7–20). The sections are preluded by an account of her home life and the circumstances leading to her becoming a governess (Chapter I); they are interrupted by several returns home for holidays (Chapter 3), for her sister's wedding (Chapter 8), and for her father's death (Chapter 18); and they are concluded by the brief account of her stay in her mother's school at A—(Chapters 21, 24, 25), and by her visit to the married Rosalie, Lady Ashby (Chapters 22, 23). The proportions of the material indicate clearly enough that this is not merely the chronicle of Agnes's life in these years. A minority of it is devoted to matters most touching her in her home life; her sister's marriage is passed over in a brief conversation with Rosalie:

'Who is she to be married to?'
'To Mr Richardson, the vicar of a neighbouring parish.'
'Is he rich?'
'No—only comfortable.'
'Is he handsome?'
'No—only decent.'
'Young?'
'No—only middling.'
'O mercy! what a wretch!'

(Chapter 8)

An exchange whose prime purpose is to display Rosalie's views on marriage, and reveals nothing of the relationship between Agnes and her sister.

Similarly Agnes's father's death is dwelt on less than the callous behaviour of Mrs Murray, who

> concluded with saying I might have the phaeton to take me to O—.
>
> 'And instead of *repining*, Miss Grey, be thankful for the *privileges* you enjoy. There's many a poor clergyman whose family would be plunged into ruin by his death; but *you*, you see, have influential friends ready to continue their patronage, and to show you every consideration.'
>
> (Chapter 18)

Anne Brontë's business in the novel is with the society and attitudes she can examine through Agnes, rather than with Agnes herself. The examination becomes more subtle and complex (though one would never call it deep), as the novel goes on. The moral weight clearly regulates the shape not only of the whole but of its parts. Agnes's troubles with the Bloomfields occupy three chapters only; her stay with the Murrays, thirteen. What looks like disproportion results in balance, and shows the modest discretion of the author, as well as the purpose guiding her. Anne Brontë begins with the straightforwardly preposterous standards of the Bloomfields, who see no wrong in allowing a frustrated child to 'spit in the faces of those who incurred her displeasure' (Chapter 3); in encouraging a seven-year-old boy to kick not only the dog, but his governess; and who consider tormenting animals a child's legitimate amusement. Even with the Bloomfields, however, the rendering of character is convincing:

> 'Damme, but the lad has some spunk in him too! Curse me, if ever I saw a nobler little scoundrel than that! He's beyond petticoat government already: —by G—he defies mother, granny, governess, and all!'
>
> (Chapter 5)

and the reasoning perversely ingenious:

> 'I think,' said she, 'a child's amusement is scarcely to be weighed against the welfare of a soulless brute.'
>
> 'But, for the child's own sake, it ought not to be encouraged to such amusements,' answered I, as meekly as I could, to make up for such unusual pertinacity. 'Blessed are the merciful, for they shall obtain mercy.'

'Oh, of course! but that refers to our conduct towards each other.'

'The merciful man shows mercy to his beast,' I ventured to add.

'I think *you* have not shown much mercy,' replied she, with a short, bitter laugh; 'killing the poor birds by wholesale, in that shocking manner, and putting the dear boy to such misery, for a mere whim!'

(Chapter 5)

The events at the Bloomfields' are so startling, and often shocking, that three chapters spent on them are enough; to continue or elaborate them would be to repeat, and to dull the effect. Once Anne Brontë has supplied an instance of the selfish and stupid father

'remember that, in future, when a decent dish leaves this table, they shall not *touch* it in the kitchen. Remember *that*, Mrs Bloomfield!'

(Chapter 3)

and of the consequences in a selfish and stupid son; and once she has made her point about the suffering that can be inflicted by both upon the helpless and the dependent, their use is over. Anne Brontë recognizes also that the grotesque is incapable of growth, and so moves her heroine away forthwith from a household of grotesques.

The transition to Horton is both smooth and artistic. Mood and themes are carried over. When Agnes first arrives at Horton, she is in charge of a family whose two youngest members are barbarians of a larger growth; John is 'rough as a young bear, boisterous, unruly, unprincipled, untaught, unteachable' and Charles 'only active in doing mischief, and only clever in inventing falsehoods' (Chapter 7). Though Anne Brontë wisely wastes no time on Agnes's tussles with them, which must repeat her tussles with the Bloomfields, their unpleasing presence connects Horton with the earlier section, while their speedy departure prepares for something new.[2]

The Murray girls are more mature and consequently more complex. Through them the novel moves on to consider not only the effects of negligent upbringing on behaviour, but the young person's own application of the deficient principles he has been given. The young boys having gone to school, the story concentrates on Rosalie, the most brilliant of the family, and the greatest disaster. The truths she exemplifies require a series of events, not mere isolated anecdotes, hence the greater length devoted to the telling. The story follows her 'coming-out' into society, her successes, her admirers, her betrothal to Sir Thomas Ashby, her encouragement and rejection of the clergyman Mr Hatfield, her attempt to captivate the curate Mr Weston, her wedding, and finally her married life. Anne Brontë firmly follows her on her career even after it has effectively ceased to be Agnes's, and drives home her message dramatically when Agnes visits Rosalie a year after her marriage (Chapter 22), to see the frustration and boredom to which her ambitions have led her. With this episode the social wheel has come full circle, Agnes Grey's function as narrator has been fulfilled, and the novel has completed its course. Rosalie has now become the parent, in her own household ruined by false values, with an unwanted child about to grow up to become, inevitably, another victim of its circumstances, as its mother has been. The situation is now seen from the mother's view:

> 'What pleasure can I have in seeing a girl grow up to eclipse me, and enjoy those pleasures I am forever debarred from? But supposing I could be so generous as to take delight in this, still it is *only* a child; and I can't centre all my hopes in a child; that is only one degree better than devoting oneself to a dog. And as for all the goodness and wisdom you have been trying to instil into me—that is all very right and proper, I dare say; and if I were some twenty years older, I might fructify by it; but people must enjoy themselves when they're young—and if others won't let them—why, they must hate them for it!'
>
>   (Chapter 23)

The final episode, which settles Agnes in the situation she merits, drives home by contrast the points made at Ashby Park, and gains its power as much from this function, as for the happiness it brings to Agnes.

By contrast with her sisters', Anne Brontë's characters seem unsubtle. Though remarkably vigorous and memorable (considering how concisely they make their effects), they undoubtedly lack the strong flavour of Charlotte's, or the sublimity of Emily's. They are much closer to common life than either, and, equally, much further from any easily identifiable literary influence. They all have the rather simple force and the conviction of the documentary, the kind of personality that emerges from the sociological survey rather than the literary imagination. Excluding Mr Weston, they are of two separate kinds: those who form Agnes's family, and those whom she encounters away from home. The differences are of attitude as well as function and treatment, and indicate once more where Anne Brontë's interests lie. She wastes little time on the Grey family, large though it must figure in Agnes's mind. Clearly she could, without destroying the balance of the book, delineate the elder sister Mary more clearly, or spend more time on the mother, but to do so would alter the tone, since these characters are conceived in a different spirit from the rest. Their purpose also is different. They are the first on whom the candid Agnes exercises her judgement for the reader's benefit, thereby gaining the reader's confidence in her. Since we recognize how justly and acutely she assesses those who are virtuous in themselves, in circumstances we can readily enter into, whom we can readily recognize for ourselves, we are prepared to trust her summings-up of strangers, whose actions might well seem close to incredible. Agnes's family are not so much the stuff of nineteenth-century fiction, as of the eighteenth-century essay:

> my father was completely overwhelmed by the calamity—health, strength, and spirits sunk beneath the blow; and he never wholly recovered them. In vain my mother strove to cheer him by appealing to his piety, to his courage, to his affection for herself and us. That very affection was his greatest torment: it was for our sakes he had so ardently longed to increase his fortune—it was our interest that had lent such brightness to his hopes, and that imparted such bitterness to his present distress.
>
> (Chapter I)

The eighteenth-century note is no disadvantage: Agnes analysing her father is as reliable as Fielding analysing Squire Allworthy, or Dr Johnson summarizing Rasselas. The note persists when the analysis is more acute and verges on the humorous:

> My mother like most active, managing women, was not gifted with very active daughters; for this reason—that being so clever and diligent herself, she was never tempted to trust her affairs to a deputy, but on the contrary, was willing to act and think for others as well as for number one.
>
> (Chapter I)

Like the essayists, she reveals no more of the character than is perceptible to the intelligent observer, and has no occasion to go deeper. Her father's sufferings, even though they hasten his death, receive no more analysis than the above. Anne Brontë is happy, however, to allow dialogue to suggest relationships and underlying characteristics, and can do so economically and pleasantly, though she has no intention of using it, like Emily Brontë, for characters' deliberate self-revelation. The suggestion of cross-purposes, and modes of thought, is neatly done when Mrs Grey suggests that Mary should try to sell some of her drawings, while Agnes is preoccupied with her own plan to become a governess:

> 'I wish *I* could do something,' said I.
> 'You, Agnes! well, who knows? You draw pretty well too; if you choose some simple piece for your subject, I dare say you will be able to produce something we shall be proud to exhibit.'
>
> (Chapter I)

The atmosphere at home is admirably created, providing the settled existence behind Agnes which makes her resilient in the face of her astonishing experiences, so much more realistic than those in *Jane Eyre* or *Villette*, whose heroines Charlotte Brontë deliberately deprives of the refuge of a safe home. Economically, Anne Brontë continues to epitomize Agnes's home in her mother. She is the main speaker in the opening chapters, and the one who remains at the end, when, elder sister married, Agnes resigns her post to help her now widowed mother run her school. She represents a norm of good sense and right feeling, little emphasized but impressive, which prevents the disproportion of a world full of vice and folly, which would result from dwelling wholly on the families who employ Agnes.

Edward Weston, curate of Horton, on the other hand, is possibly the shadowiest hero ever invented by a woman novelist. If Agnes were the all-absorbing heroine, this would be a very serious charge. In fact, though he cannot rouse much interest in the reader, or demand long consideration, he does adequately what he is called upon to do. He is primarily the doer of good deeds in a naughty world, the only well-principled person of her own class, other than her family, whom Agnes meets. He functions always as a moral force. He is the immediate contrast to the worldly and careless clergyman Mr Hatfield, and, even as the man Agnes loves, what are stressed are his moral qualities:

> I could think of him day and night; and I could feel that he was worthy to be thought of. Nobody knew him as I did; nobody could appreciate him as I did.
>
> (Chapter 17)

Lack of information is a dramatic asset when he is marked down by Rosalie as her last victim. The reader, like Agnes, knows his virtue, but has no way of knowing his emotional temperament, or how he will respond to Rosalie's advances. While the end of the story is certain—by the convention of the novel he will marry Agnes—there is no way of telling whether he will succumb to Rosalie and then, disillusioned, recover, or whether he will be acute enough to resist her.[3] A modest originality of Mr Weston's is to be an early instance of the unhandsome hero. The man 'a little, a very little, above the middle size' with 'his face too square for beauty', eyebrows 'too projecting' and eyes 'brown in colour, not large, and somewhat deepest, but strikingly brilliant' (Chapter II) is the counterpart of a heroine with 'marked features, pale hollow cheek, and ordinary dark brown hair', just as Mr Rochester is the counterpart of Jane.[4] Anne Brontë does here, calmly, without any sense in the writing that she is being novel, what Charlotte Brontë afterwards does with panache—a man who has no charms save in the eye of the narrator.

All the other characters are knaves or fools in some degree, even the children. Their failings are what justify their literary existence. Such a statement suggests that *Agnes Grey* must be either a satire, or a work of very limited interest. The nature of Agnes herself prevents it being the first, while the functions of the other characters prevent its being the second. Like the Grey family, the rest are seen only from outside, by the intelligent observer Agnes, whose author never allows her to guess at or speculate on the variety of impulses and motives which produce the behaviour she observes. Anne Brontë never causes the reader to worry what there can have been in common between Mr and Mrs Murray, for example, to cause them to marry, nor suggests how they may behave to each other in situations where Agnes herself could not observe them. She does not resolve the difficulty of how a selfish woman can endure the company of her own intolerable children. But she chronicles with such precision that the immediate incident rings so true as not to invite such speculation. Anne, like Emily, observes personalities, and allows them to expose themselves; she does not analyse or dissect; a feature which reveals that she is closer to Emily in this matter than to Charlotte, who is as much concerned with interior causes as with effects. The purpose of Anne Brontë's characterization is not psychological, but social. Actions and attributes are selected to lead the reader to consider their social and personal consequences, not their causes.

It is therefore wise of her to begin with the inhabitants of Wellwood. The reader's natural tendency with a child is to consider it as a being with a potential, but no past, who is very much the direct consequences of the influences it feels. The distasteful Bloomfield brood—Tom, Mary Ann, and Fanny—are presented firmly as the results of irresponsible overindulgence, to be judged themselves for conscious vices, and to cause judgement to be made both on their parents, and, by extension, on the grossly deficient moral and social standards by which the parents live. Good care is taken that they shall not be pitied as victims, either of the system or each other: Tom Bloomfield, enjoying brutality and torment, is his uncle Robson in miniature; Mary Ann, whom he bullies, is deliberately, systematically and inflexibly perverse, and the bad habits of both, and of the even younger Fanny, are such as to rouse more revulsion in the reader than in the narrator. Agnes herself and the nurserymaid Betty (who puts in a brief appearance in Chapter 3) prevent the reader from supposing that the children suffer from lack of affection, since it is offered and rejected. Anne Brontë clearly believes in original sin, as well as natural good, and in training as the very necessary force that will turn a child into a good man. The Bloomfield children's purpose, since they occupy only four hair-raising chapters, is to prepare the way for the Murrays, a more subtle and exhaustive study of the corruption of the individual, and the effects of wrong training on a faulty nature. Agnes, brooding on her charges, remarks:

> the children would, in time, become more humanized: every month would contribute to make them some little wiser, and, consequently, more manageable; for a child of nine or ten, as frantic and ungovernable as these at six and seven would be a maniac.
>
> (Chapter 3)

The Murrays, in their early teens, bear her out, and the reader, when he meets them, is prepared to regard them in the same way as the Bloomfields, looking only to the consequences they bring about, not to what caused them to become what they are.

The parents of these unhappy offspring are revealed with the same documentary precision, though, because they impinge less on Agnes, and are less to the purpose, more briefly. Again the eighteenth-century note is heard, and the characters of Mr and Mrs Bloomfield, the Grandmother, and Uncle Robson seem true to type without ever seeming trite. They are revealed through the individual, small, significant encounter, and usually through dialogue. Mr Bloomfield suddenly and arbitrarily interrupts the narrative, just as he suddenly and arbitrarily descends on Agnes and his children, to abuse them and her and depart; Uncle Robson, a more positive evil though a temporary one, makes his devastating comment on his nephew, Tom, raging over the loss of his birds' nest, and departs likewise:

> 'Curse me, if ever I saw a nobler little scoundrel than that! He's beyond petticoat government already! —By G— he defies

mother, granny, governess, and all! Ha, ha, ha! Never mind, Tom, I'll get you another brood tomorrow.'

(Chapter 5)

Mrs Bloomfield on the other hand makes an impressive first appearance doing nothing; all the while Agnes wrestles with tough, cold, meat, with her hands numb from five hours' exposure to the bitter wind, what is being sensed is the tough, cold, numb Mrs Bloomfield silently watching her.

The handling of the convincingly unreasonable characters here leads forward to Horton, where the characters are to be unreasonable in ways more elaborate, and seemingly more like what usually appear in a novel. In the background are the neglecting father, and the worldly mother, seeing only what is to her daughter's social and financial advantage, bending all her efforts to an early and profitable marriage; in the foreground the two contrasting young women, the hoyden and the coquette; and attending on Rosalie an assortment of suitors, amongst whom the brutish and successful landowner contrasts, in his turn, with the aspiring social climber, the rector. Here also Anne Brontë successfully imposes her own tone, and, while using the stuff of convention, sees it not at all in the conventional way, contriving never to slip into the merely grotesque on the one hand, or on the other to allow herself or the reader to be seduced by the charm of what is inescapably reprehensible. The personality and position of Agnes herself imposes proportion, since what looms largest to her is also what matters most to the story and theme. The method is economical in itself, and performed with natural economy. The characterization here has the same verve as at Wellwood, but is far more varied in its methods. The least significant personalities are suggested with splendid precision. The setting, the kind of character, the cool justice which is accorded them, the humane partly-involved narrator, the mingling of humour with instruction, all suggest, not another of the Brontës, but Trollope. While it is clear that his handling of elaborate ecclesiastical politics and the edges of high society is beyond her, so are her just proportioning of means to her end, her impulse to understate rather than elaborate her points, beyond Trollope. Mr Murray for instance is only of concern as the father figure for an unsatisfactory family in general, and as the one who authorizes and condones Matilda in her hunting and swearing. Agnes never [sees] him 'to speak to' (Chapter 12) as she says, but 'the figure of a tall stout gentleman with scarlet cheeks and crimson nose' (Chapter 7), precisely noted at the beginning of her account of the family, remains firmly fixed in the reader's mind. Mrs Murray, more important since her influence is upon the more important daughter Rosalie, is permitted to impress herself by speech, by quietly devastating self-exposure:

'I have hitherto found all the governesses, even the very best of them, faulty in this particular. They wanted that meek and quiet spirit which St Matthew, or some of them, says is better than the putting on of apparel—you will know the passage to which I allude, for you are a clergyman's daughter.'

(Chapter 7)

Her moral values, her self-satisfaction, her relationship to her governess need no more explanation. On the rare occasions when it is necessary to suggest her motives, the method is equally laconic:

having notwithstanding the disadvantages of a country life so satisfactorily disposed of her elder daughter, the pride of her heart, [she] had begun seriously to turn her attention to the younger.

(Chapter 18)

'satisfactorily' suggests her own opinion, 'disposed' suggests Agnes's; while the conventional phrase 'pride of her heart' takes on a new richness applied to a relationship which has displayed all too much 'pride' and a total lack of 'heart'.

The younger daughter Matilda contrasts with her sister (her main function in the novel), demonstrating that, while to be sophisticated like Rosalie is unadmirable, to lack the quality may be, not admirable, but merely uncouth; to be deceitful like Rosalie is wrong, but merely to be frank in admitting is but little better:

'I pretended to want to save it, [a leveret killed by her dog] as it was so glaringly out of season; but I was better pleased to see it killed.'

(Chapter 18)

Anne Brontë's art shows in Matilda, as so often elsewhere, in her discretion and restraint. Though Matilda is reportedly foulmouthed, the reader hears very little of her, since to do so would make her too uncouth to be an impressive opposite to Rosalie. Her stable language is heard no more once its comic point has been made:

'I'll never say a wicked word again, if you'll only listen to me, and tell Rosalie to hold her confounded tongue.'

(Chapter 9)

Rosalie is almost as much the heart of the novel as Agnes herself. She embodies the most serious moral preoccupations, she is the most closely–observed, her career is the most complete, she is the most self-exposing, and she is the object of the most serious and complete concern not only of the narrator but of the author. Whereas Agnes understates her own affairs of the heart (out of diffidence and modesty), Anne Brontë allows no such consideration to prevent the reader from observing Rosalie at all the most memorable points in her career. This career extends from the childhood period, when she is the product of her environment and education, through that when, as a young woman, she chooses her course for herself, to her married life when she experiences the consequences of her conduct. The account of a governess is the ideal one for mapping such a course. Agnes is intimate enough for her pupil to confide in her, but not enough respected either to influence or repress her. Hence Rosalie explains herself as does no other character, laying bare her opinions (she has very few feelings) on what she has already done, and her plans for what she proposes to do. Frequently these opinions and plans loom larger than the events connected with them: for instance, the reader has Rosalie's account of her coming-out ball (Chapter 9), not the ball itself; her words immediately after being married (Chapter 18), but not the wedding. The disproportion between the events and the importance they assume in her career (the coming-out ball takes more space than the wedding), allows the moral point to make itself, with very little help from Agnes as commentator. Equally pertinent is the disproportion between characters, revealed through how Rosalie regards them. Her husband, Sir Thomas Ashby, is mentioned no more than is essential for the reader's benefit—he is 'the greatest scamp in Christendom' and 'any woman of common decency' is 'a world too good for him' (Chapter 14) —but the rector Mr Hatfield looms large in the narrative, both in her conversation and account of her thoughts, and in events in which they both take part. Rosalie is indeed the main reason why events and characters appear, even when she is not present.[5]

The ways in which Rosalie is presented show considerable assurance and unobtrusive skill. Since Anne Brontë's purposes do not include psychological development and interpretation, an opening description which fixes permanently the main features of a personality serves her well. Rosalie receives the most comprehensive and significant one in the novel. Her looks, the obvious beginning of a description, are a significant one here, revealing that this young lady's face is her fortune. Though such a character is not unusual, the account is far from conventional, and has the astringent edge of truth, which renders vivid both the subject and the speaker:

---

on a further acquaintance, she gradually laid aside her airs, and in time, became as deeply attached to me as it was possible for her to be to one of my character and position: for she seldom lost sight, for above half-an-hour at a time, of the fact of my being a hireling, and a poor curate's daughter.

(Chapter 7)

Once she is thus established, she makes most of her effects by speech, of which she has more than any other single person (excluding Agnes herself and the other temporary narrator, Nancy Brown). Like so many of Anne Brontë's effects, her speech is successful in context, being completely appropriate and exactly serving its purpose; but it contains much less that is immediately striking in extract. Self-exposure, by a frankness that ironically reveals more to Agnes and the reader than she intends, is its most frequent feature:

'Brown said that she was sure no gentleman could set eyes on me without falling in love that minute; and so I may be allowed to be a little vain. I know you think me a shocking, conceited, frivolous girl, but then you know, I don't attribute it *all* to my personal attractions: I give some praise to the hairdresser, and some to my exquisitely lovely dress—you must see it tomorrow— white gauze over pink satin . . . and so *sweetly* made! and a necklace and bracelet of beautiful, large pearls!'

'I have no doubt you looked very charming; but should that delight you so very much?'

'Oh, no! . . . not that alone: but then, I was so much admired; and I made so *many* conquests in that one night—you'd be astonished to hear—'

'But what good will they do you?'

'What good! Think of any woman asking that!'

'Well, I should think one conquest would be enough, and too much, unless the subjugation were mutual.'

(Chapter 9)

The hints here of the maid Brown's idiom which opens the speech, the limited wit in Rosalie which acknowledges the hairdresser's and costumier's help, but entertainingly misunderstands Agnes's question 'should that delight you?', and cannot save her from the vulgarism of 'conquests' (emphasized by Agnes's literal and polysyllabic periphrasis, 'subjugation'— recalling Charlotte Brontë's humour); all these are neatly and unobtrusively suggested without either idiosyncratic diction or unnatural idiom.[6]

The method which serves the Rosalie of the early chapters works just as well for the dissatisfied married woman as for the pleasure-loving girl. Absence of proper feeling shows itself in her letter to Agnes (Chapter 21), where she speaks in the same offhand tone of her child, her dog, and her pictures:

> 'I forget whether you like babies; if you do, you may have the pleasure of seeing mine . . . the most charming child in the world, no doubt . . . and you shall see my poodle too, a splendid little charmer imported from Paris, and two fine Italian paintings of great value . . . I forget the artist.'
>
> (Chapter 21)

Her acute, though faulty, reasoning is obvious again in her confidences, where this time Agnes's comment is an unspoken one:

> 'as soon as he heard we were there, he came up under pretence of visiting his brother, and either followed me, like a shadow, wherever I went, or met me, like a reflection, at every turn. You needn't look so shocked, Miss Grey; I was very discreet, I assure you; but, you know, one can't help being admired.'
>
> (Chapter 22)

Though static, the character is by no means elementary. Anne Brontë, having established the deficiencies, allows the considerable charm of youth and high spirits, and gives Rosalie all the assets deriving from doing what the reader longs to have done—putting the pretentious Mr Hatfield in his place. Similarly she can let Rosalie infuse some transitory excitement into the story by attempting to charm Mr Weston: her charm and intelligence have been just enough to make Agnes's anxiety seem justified, and the chance that Mr Weston may succumb seem one worth considering.

Mr Hatfield himself is a small but thoroughly adequate piece of work. His purposes as the foppish, ambitious clergyman, with no sense of his calling, are easily fulfilled by lively details of his behaviour:

> [Mr Hatfield] would come sailing up the aisle, or rather sweeping along like a whirlwind, with his rich silk gown flying behind him, and rustling against the pew doors, mount the pulpit like a conqueror ascending his triumphal car; then sinking on the velvet cushion in an attitude of studied grace, remain in silent prostration for a certain time.
>
> (Chapter 10)

But such details as this, and kicking Nancy Brown's cat out of his way, do not suggest the power and originality of the scene, reported verbatim by Rosalie (Chapter 14), of his astonishing proposal to her, which proceeds by way of conventional protestation, through astonishment and chagrin, to repressed rage and a direct *tu quoque* and threat of blackmail to protect wounded pride.

The principles of economy and the strong sense of means to an end that dictate the personality and role of the narrator, the shape of the whole, and the handling of characters, determine also the selection and manipulation of material within the individual scenes, and the style. It is even more plain here that Anne Brontë is an author whose effects are made by accumulation and inter-relation of simple details, very simply expressed, whose power is largely lost when they are seen in isolation. Her greatest single asset, apart from the handling of Agnes herself, is, as has already been examined, her use of dialogue. As well as revealing personality and exposing standards and lapses, speech is often used as an economical and dramatic means to other ends. There are occasional intrusions of transitory characters like Mr Smith 'the draper, grocer and tea-dealer of the village' (Chapter I) whose gig takes Agnes to her first post. His comment:

> 'It's a coldish mornin' for you, Miss Agnes, and a darksome un too; but we's, happen, get to yon' spot afore there comes much rain to signify.'

and the laconic little dialogue that follows, create an accurate and atmospheric vignette without holding up the narrative, and create variety between the author's account of her home, and that of the Bloomfields which is to follow. Nancy Brown's long account of her spiritual troubles in Chapter 11 is another instance of speech whose end is structural. It again forms a welcome break in Agnes's story, and provides information it is not in her power to give, in a novel, compact, and racy way. While so long an account is not naturalistic, Anne Brontë balances most professionally the demands of easy reading with keeping up a convincing dialect, wisely relying more on idiom than on phonetic reproduction:

> 'After he was gone, Hannah Rogers, one o' th' neighbours came in and wanted me to help her to wash. I telled her I couldn't just then, for I hadn't set on th' potaties for th' dinner, nor washed up th' breakfast stuff yet. So then she began a calling me for my nasty, idle ways. I was a little bit vexed at first; but I never said nothing wrong to her: I only telled her, like all in a quiet way, 'a I'd had th' new parson to see me; but I'd get done as quick as ever

I could, an' then come an' help her. So then she softened down.'
                                    (Chapter II)

One hears Yorkshire speech as effectively here as in the much less decipherable Joseph of *Wuthering Heights*.

Scenery, setting, and the weather are plainly elements of situation as important to Anne Brontë as to her sisters. Like them she feels a whole scene through its central emotion, without ever suggesting sentimentality or the pathetic fallacy. Frequent and delicate notice of details of setting, of the weather, the seasons, or the passage of time, all vivify both the action and the subdued personality of Agnes herself. Here Anne Brontë rightly feels confident that mere allusion will evoke a response, without relying on description. She can be vivid and oddly moving with the most commonplace materials, precisely because what she uses is so familiar that she can depend upon the reader's response. Agnes, arriving exhausted at Horton Lodge after a winter day's travelling, where she gets no proper welcome, goes up to her room:

> Then, having broken my long fast on a cup of tea, and a little thin bread and butter, I sat down beside the small, smouldering fire, and amused myself with a hearty fit of crying.
>   (Chapter 7)

Anne Brontë always thus underplays rather than overplays her hand, marking the story's most moving moments by bringing some small detail into sharp focus, as in this brief account of Agnes's first journey from home:

> We crossed the valley, and began to ascend the opposite hill. As we were toiling up, I looked back again: there was the village spire, and the old grey parsonage beyond it, basking in a slanting beam of sunshine—it was but a sickly ray, but the village and surrounding hills were all in sombre shade, and I hailed the wandering beam as a propitious omen to my home. With clasped hands, I fervently implored a blessing on its inhabitants, and hastily turned away; for I saw the sunshine was departing; and I carefully avoided another glance, lest I should see it in gloomy shadow like the rest of the landscape.
>   (Chapter I)

There is a deliberate rejection here of the significant or symbolic, for the sunshine moves naturally with the clouds; the significance is only what Agnes imagines, while what she describes has all the charm of reality. Like her sisters, Anne Brontë has also a strong sense of time passing. Each event in the story is precisely placed in its season, usually by its month.[7] In a story where the most significant happenings will almost certainly take place on Sundays—when going to church involves meeting the clergyman—such care might be imposed rather than voluntary. But Anne Brontë can delineate time passing like a prose Tennyson; the passage where Agnes at Ashby Park waits and muses in her sitting-room is almost her *Mariana*:

> I sat musing on Lady Ashby's past and present condition; and on what little information I had obtained respecting Mr Weston, and the small chance there was of ever seeing or hearing anything more of him throughout my quiet, drab-colour life, which, henceforth, seemed to offer no alternative between positive rainy days and days of dull, grey clouds without downfall.
>
> At length, however, I began to weary of my thoughts, and to wish I knew where to find the library my hostess had spoken of, and to wonder whether I was to remain there, doing nothing till bedtime.
>
> As I was not rich enough to possess a watch, I could not tell how time was passing, except by observing the slowly lengthening shadows from the window, which presented a side view, including a corner of the park, a clump of trees, whose topmost branches had been colonized by an innumerable company of noisy rooks, and a high wall with a massive wooden gate, no doubt communicating with the stable yard, as a broad carriage-road swept up to it from the park. The shadow of this wall soon took possession of the whole of this ground as far as I could see, forcing the golden sunlight to retreat inch by inch, and at last take refuge in the very tops of the trees. At last, even they were left in shadow—the shadow of the distant hills, or of the earth itself; and, in sympathy for the busy citizens of the rookery, I regretted to see their habitation, so lately bathed in glorious light, reduced to the sombre, work-a-day hue of the lower world, or of my own world within. For a moment, such birds as soared above the might still receive the lustre on their wings, which imparted to their sable plumage the hue and brilliance of deep red gold; at last, that too departed. Twilight came stealing on— the rooks became more quiet—I became more weary, and wished I were going home tomorrow.

(Chapter 22)

As this passage and the previous ones reveal, expression is wholly ruled by what she has to say. The demands of sound, rhythm, or the well-wrought period do not concern her. She does not reject the oddly-used word 'basking', in the second passage; nor does she acknowledge, in the third, that the rhythm of the third sentence concludes at the words 'wooden gate': completeness demands the rather awkwardly attached dependent phrase and clause beginning at 'no doubt communication . . .', and completeness justifies its presence and its form. These sensitive and even lyrical descriptions all belong to Agnes, and bear on her role in the narrative. She is passive and sensitive, a central perception more fine than any other, and so a most accurate measurement of the other characters, though she is not at all the most absorbing interest for the reader.

On its small scale Agnes Grey has much in common with *Mansfield Park*, and Agnes herself with Fanny Price, who is in a similar position, has a rather similar nature, and performs the same functions. Anne Brontë resembles her sisters only where material is concerned (only occasionally do her methods suggest Emily), and resembles the eighteenth century in the type of characterization and the firm mortality; the Victorians she suggests are those very different from the Brontës, Mrs Gaskell and Trollope; while a remarkable affinity exists between her and that other modest writer, of deep personal religion, pervadingly humble subjects, and a deceptively simple, literal style—Mark Rutherford.

NOTES

1. Mrs. Robinson is better known as the object of Branwell Brontë's ill-founded passion than as the original of Anne's portrait, which is considerably more cooly damning than anything in Branwell's history, though that also indicates a true mother of the daughter figured forth in Rosalie.

2. The two girls also are mere schoolgirls at first, Matilda only thirteen, and Rosalie, at sixteen, still 'something of a romp' (Chapter 7), who has yet to grow up into the accomplished coquette.

3. Any treatment of Weston such as that of Mr. Rochester and Blanche Ingram would, though possibly creating more absorbing personalities, be to no useful end, since the movement at this point cannot turn away from Rosalie herself (the 'Blanche Ingram' of the episode) who is being swept on to uncongenial wedlock.

4. He and Mr. Rochester may well have a similar source, sharing as well as

looks a fine voice, while at one point Mr Weston even uses a Rochester image

> 'The human heart is like india-rubber; a little swells it, but a great deal will not burst it. (Chapter 12)   anticipating Mr Rochester's declaring himself as 'hard and tough as an India-rubber ball: pervious, though, through a chink or two still, and with one sentient point in the middle of the lump.' (*Jane Eyre*, Chapter 14.)

5.   A striking instance is in Agnes's visit to the old blind woman Nancy Brown, where Nancy's long account of her religious doubts dwells as much on Mr. Hatfield's deficiencies as on Mr. Weston's excellences; the former need to be known in order to gauge the falseness of his sentiment to Rosalie, the latter to create anxiety about her attempts, as she herself says, to 'fix' him (Chapter 15), though it also obviously reveals him as a fitting husband for Agnes.

6.   Such success with plain language is one outside the power of either Charlotte or Emily Brontë, and places Anne rather with Mrs. Gaskell or Trollope.

7.   Rosalie's 'coming-out' ball takes place on 3 January, Agnes visits Nancy in the third week in February, Mr. Weston gives her primroses at the end of March, Mr. Hatfield's courtship, refusal, and Rosalie's change to Mr. Weston proceed day by day, and she is married on 1 June.

SANDRA M. GILBERT AND SUSAN GUBAR

The Buried Life of Lucy Snowe

My very chains and I grew friends,
So much a long communion tends
To make us what we are. . . .
        —Lord Byron

The prisoner in solitary confinement, the toad in the block of
marble, all in time shape themselves to their lot.
        —Charlotte Brontë

One need not be a Chamber—to be Haunted—
One need not be a House—
The Brain has Corridors—surpassing
Material Place—
        —Emily Dickinson

The cage of myself clamps shut.
My words turn the lock
. . . .
I am the lackey who "follows orders."
I have not got the authority.
        —Erica Jong

From *The Madwoman in the Attic* by Sandra M Gilbert and Susan Gubar, (New Haven: Yale University Press, 1984): pp. 399–440. Reprinted by permission.

Villette is in many ways Charlotte Brontë's most overtly and despairingly feminist novel. *The Professor* and *Shirley*, as we have seen, at least pretended to have other intentions, disguising their powerful preoccupations with the anxieties of femaleness behind cool, pseudomasculine façades; and *Jane Eyre*, though rebelliously feminist in its implications, used a sort of fairy tale structure to enable the novelist to conceal even from herself her deepening pessimism about woman's place in man's society. But Lucy Snowe, *Villette's* protagonist-narrator, older and wiser than any of Brontë's other heroines, is from first to last a woman *without*—outside society, without parents or friends, without physical or mental attractions, without money or confidence or health—and her story is perhaps the most moving and terrifying account of female deprivation ever written.

Silent, invisible, at best an inoffensive shadow, Lucy Snowe has no patrimony and no expectations, great or little. Even her creator appears to find her "morbid and weak,"[1] frigid, spiritless: some "subtlety of thought made me decide upon giving her a cold name," she told her publisher.[2] A progressive deterioration in spirit and exuberance from Frances Henri and Jane Eyre, who demand equality and life, to Caroline Helstone, who rarely voices her protest, is completed by Lucy's submission and silence, as if Charlotte Brontë equates maturity with an aging process that brings women only a stifling sense of despair. Indeed the movement of the novels suggests that escape becomes increasingly difficult as women internalize the destructive strictures of patriarchy. Locked into herself, defeated from the start, Lucy Snowe is tormented by the realization that she has bought survival at the price of never fully existing, escaped pain by retreating behind a dull, grave camouflage. Haunted by the persons she might have been, she has been dispossessed not only of meanings and goals, but also of her own identity and power. How can she escape the person she has become?

Villette is the last of a series of the writer's fictional attempts to come to terms with her own loveless existence, and specifically with her sorrow at the loss of M. Héger's friendship. Her love for this Brussels schoolteacher ended first in a kind of solitary confinement imposed on Brontë by his wife, and finally in his refusal to respond to Brontë's letters from England. One of her earliest and most plainly autobiographical poems, "Frances," describes not only the desolation that Frances Henri experiences in *The Professor* but Brontë's own profound feelings of exclusion. The heroine's life is a kind of living death:

> For me the universe is dumb,
>   Stone-deaf, and blank, and wholly blind;
> Life I must bound, existence sum

> In the strait limits of one mind;
> That mind my own. Oh! narrow cell;
> Dark—imageless—a living tomb!
> There must I sleep, there wake and dwell
> Content,—with palsy, pain, and gloom.[3]

Lucy Snowe, like Frances in the poem and also, to some extent, like Frances Henri before her marriage, is bound by the limits of her own mind—a dark and narrow cell. Living inside this tomb, she discovers that it is anything but imageless; it is a chamber of terrible visions, not the least of which is that of being buried alive.

That Matthew Arnold, responding to Brontë's hunger, rebellion, and rage, found all this eminently disagreeable is understandable, although—perhaps *because*—the year before the publication of *Villette*, he wrote a poem very much about Lucy's dilemma. "The Buried Life" laments the falseness of an existence divorced from the hidden self. Like Lucy, Arnold knows that many conceal their true feelings for fear they will be met with indifference. Both Arnold and Lucy describe the discrepancy between a dumb, blank life and the hidden, passionate center of being. But the difference between the two views is instructive. For while Lucy's repression is a response to a society cruelly indifferent to women, Arnold claims that the genuine self is buried in all people. Perhaps this explains why the anguished horror of Lucy's experience is absent from Arnold's poem. His is a metaphysical elegy, hers an obsessively personal one. Lucy feels herself confined to a prison cell, while Arnold describes an active life in the world even if it is a life cut off from the forceful river that is the true self. Again, where Lucy rebels against confinement, Arnold philosophically claims that perhaps all is for the best. Fate, he implies, has decreed that the true self be buried so that it cannot be subverted by the conscious will, and thus, he suggests, nature is working benevolently for all.

Arnold is articulating the vague and ultimately optimistic *Weltschmerz* so popular in early and mid-nineteenth-century poetry. Like Byron, Shelley, and Wordsworth, he laments his distance from "the soul's subterranean depth," while holding out the possibility that there are times when "what we mean, we say, and what we would, we know."[4] But as a woman Brontë cannot fully participate in the Romantic conventions of what amounted by her time to a fully developed literary tradition. The male Romantics, having moved independently in society, condemned the trivial world of getting and spending, while Brontë's exclusion from social and economic life precluded her free rejection of it. On the contrary, many of her female characters yearn to enter the competitive marketplace reviled by the poets. Thus, where the male Romantics glorified the "buried life" to an ontology, Brontë explores the mundane facts of homelessness, poverty, physical unattractiveness, and sexual discrimination or stereotyping that impose self-burial on women. While male poets like Arnold express their desire to experience an inner and more valid self, Brontë describes the pain of women who are restricted to just this private realm. Instead of seeking and celebrating the buried self, these women feel victimized by it; they long, instead, for actualization in the world.

By focusing on a female subject, too, Brontë implicitly criticizes the way in which her male counterparts have found solace for their spiritual yearnings in the limpid look and the tender touch. In "The Buried Life," as in many of his other poems, Arnold implores his female listener to turn her eyes on his so he can read her inmost soul. But the skeptical female reader knows Arnold will see there his own reflection.[5] Thus, confronting and rejecting the egotistical sublime, Brontë questions the tradition Arnold inherits from Wordsworth, for both poets seek escape from the dreary intercourse of daily life through the intercession of a girl, image and source of the poets' faith. Brontë's aversion to such a solution explains the numerous echoes in *Villette* of Wordsworth's "Lucy Gray" and of his "Lucy" poems. Living hidden among untrodden ways, wandering alone on a snowy moonlit moor, disappearing in the wild storm, both Lucy and Lucy Gray had functioned for the poet much as his sister did in "Tintern Abbey," as emblems of the calm and peace that nature brings. Here and elsewhere in her fiction, however, Brontë reinterprets the little-girl-lost story in order to redefine the myth from the lost girl's point of view.

Lucy Snowe is thus in important ways a parody of Lucy or Lucy Gray. Far from being nature's favorite, she seems to be one of those chosen for adversity. Instead of being blessed because she is, as Wordsworth says, "a thing that could not feel,"[6] she is damned: apparently nature *can* betray even those who love her. For in this, her last novel, Brontë explores not the redemptive but the destructive effect of the buried life on women who can neither escape by retreating into the self (since such a retreat is rejected as solipsistic) nor find a solution by dehumanizing the other into a spiritual object. Still, even if there can be no joyous celebration, not even abundant recompense, at least Brontë provides in *Villette* an honest elegy for all those women, who cannot find ways out and are robbed of their will to live. At the same time, *Villette* is also the story of the writer's way out. Implying that the female artist is as confined by male conventions as her characters are imprisoned in the institutions of a patriarchal society, Brontë considers the inadequacy of male culture in her search for a female language; her rejection of male-devised arts contributes to her extraordinary depiction of the potential dangers of the imagination for women.

* * *

From the very first sentence of *Villette*, which describes the handsome house of Lucy's godmother, it is clear that Brontë has once again created a heroine who is caught in an anomalous family position. The symbolically named Bretton house is the first of a series of female-owned and operated dwellings, an important sign that in some ways Lucy's confinement is self-administered. This is immediately substantiated by her guarded demeanor: even as she journeys from Mrs. Bretton's to Miss Marchmont's house and then to Madame Beck's school, Lucy remains taciturn and withdrawn. Yet, paradoxically, if she is more submissive than her predecessors, she is also more rebellious, refusing to be a governess because her "dimness and depression must both be voluntary."[7] Modern critics of *Villette* recognize the conflict between restraint and passion, reason and imagination within her. But its full significance depends on the ways in which the other characters in the novel are used to objectify what amounts to this protagonist's schizophrenia,[8] for Lucy Snowe exemplifies the truth of Emily Dickinson's "One need not be a Chamber—to be Haunted—" (J. 670).

Instead of participating in the life of the Brettons, Lucy watches it. The appearance of another child-visitor emphasizes her ironic detachment. Not only does Lucy feel contemptuous of six-year-old Polly's need for love and male protection—her dependence first on her father and then her enthralled attraction to Graham Bretton, an older boy incapable of returning her love—she ridicules Polly's fanatic responses and doll-like gestures, and satirizes Polly's refusal to eat, as well as her need to serve food to her father or his surrogate. Above such demonstrative displays herself, she proclaims her superiority: "I, Lucy Snowe, was calm" (chap. 3). While Polly nestles under her father's cloak or Graham's arms for protection, Lucy sneers at the girl who must "live, move and have her being in another" (chap. 3). Yet though Lucy seems determined not to exist in another's existence, we soon notice that her voyeuristic detachment defines her in terms of others as inexorably as Polly's parasitic attachments define the younger girl.

Lucy's passive calm contrasts with Polly's passionate intensity; her withdrawal with Polly's playfulness. But, as is so often the case in Brontë's fiction, these two antithetical figures have much in common. Diligent and womanly beyond their years, neat in their ways, and self-controlled in their verbal expression of emotion, both are visitors in the Bretton house, inhabiting the same chamber. That they are intimately connected becomes obvious when Lucy wants Polly to cry out at a moment of great joy so that she, Lucy, can get some relief (chap. 2). For, strangely, Lucy has discovered in Polly a representative of part of herself who "haunts" her (chap. 2) like "a small ghost" (chap. 3). Finally, she takes this ghost into her own bed to comfort her when she feels bereaved, wondering about the child's destiny, which, significantly, she imagines in terms of the humiliations and desolations that are prepared for her *own* life. As Q. D. Leavis suggests, Polly acts out all those impulses already repressed by Lucy[9] so that the two girls represent the two sides of Lucy's divided self, and they are the first of a series of such representative antagonists.

Their fates will be in some ways comparable. As if to stress this, Polly shows Lucy a book about distant countries which functions structurally—much like the book of Bewick prints introduced at the beginning of *Jane Eyre*, or *Coriolanus* in *Shirley*—to hint at future dangers. As Polly describes the desolate places, the good English missionary, the Chinese lady's bound foot, and the land of ice and snow, Lucy listens intently, because these are the trials that await those split, as she is, between passive acceptance of a limited lot and rebellious desire for a full life. The book foretells the exile both girls will eventually experience, complete with a godlike healer, specifically foreign forms of repression, and the cold that always endangers female survival. Lucy will have to seek her identity on foreign soil because she is metaphorically a foreigner even in England. Homeless, she is a woman without a country or a community, or so her subsequent status as an immigrant would seem to suggest.

On another level, moreover, Lucy's dilemma is internal, and Brontë dramatizes it again when the girl enters yet another English woman's house. The elderly invalid Miss Marchmont, a woman whose self-imposed confinement defines the tragic causes and consequences of withdrawal, serves as a monitory image. At the same time, though, alone and in mourning for her lost family, hollow-eyed Lucy already resembles her mistress, a rheumatic cripple confined within two upstairs rooms where she waits for death as a release from pain. Because Lucy prizes the morsel of affection she receives, she is almost content to subsist on an invalid's diet, almost content to *be* Miss Marchmont. Unlike Pip in *Great Expectations*, who would never consider becoming Miss Havisham (even though he pities her the living death caused by the cruel Compeyson), but very much like Anne Elliot, who identifies with the paralyzed Mrs. Smith, Lucy is acquiescent because willing "to escape occasional great agonies by submitting to a whole life of privation and small pains" (chap. 4). Her employer's self-confinement, moreover, is also a response to great pain. Miss Marchmont tells Lucy how, 30 years earlier, on a moonlit Christmas Eve, she watched by the lattice, anxiously awaiting her lover's approaching gallop and unable to speak when she saw his dead body—"that thing in the moonlight" (chap. 4). Just as Lucy's detachment is a self-sustaining response to the pain endured by the vulnerable Polly, Miss Marchmont has based a life of privation and seclusion on the disappointment of her desire when she saw her lover's corpse in the moonlight.

Nevertheless, even while her predicament implies that self-incarceration is potentially every woman's fate, Miss Marchmont's life story reverses one of Wordsworth's "Lucy" poems. In "Strange Fits of Passion Have I Known," the speaker, a horseman, gallops under the evening moon to his lover's cot, besieged by the wayward thought that she is dead. Brontë, however, approaches the event from the stationary and enclosed perspective of the waiting woman, whose worst fears are always substantiated. An emblem of the fatality of love, Miss Marchmont lives in confinement, a perpetual virgin dedicated to the memory of the lover she lost on Christmas Eve. She is in effect a nun, but a nun who receives no religious consolation, since she can neither understand nor condone the ways of God. Love, she says, has brought her pain that would have refined an amiable nature to saintliness and turned daemonic an evil spirit (chap. 4). Whether transformed into a nun or a witch, her story suggests, the woman who allows herself to experience love is betrayed and destroyed, for once her best self is buried with her love, she is condemned to endure, alone, in the tomblike cell that is her mind.

What some critics have termed the inflated diction of the Miss Marchmont section[10] is reinforced by the details Brontë uses to depict Lucy's progress on a mythic pilgrimage. It is, ironically, the icy aurora borealis that brings Lucy the energy, after she is released by Miss Marchmont's death, to "Leave this wilderness." (chap. 5). With her desolation rising before her "like a ghost" (chap. 5), Lucy possesses nothing except loathing of her past existence. The watermen fighting over her fare, the black river, the ship named *The Vivid*, the destination Boue-Marine ("ocean mud"), her remembrance of the Styx and of Charon rowing souls to the land of shades— all reflect her anxiety that the trip will end disastrously, even as they mythologize this voyage out through the unconscious toward selfhood. And it is only with this mythic sense of her quest that we can understand the almost surreal details of her arrival in *La/basse/cour*—the canals creeping like half-torpid snakes, the gray and stagnant sky, the single trustworthy Englishman who guides her part of the way through the little city (*Villette*), and the two lecherous men who pursue her, driving her deep into the old, narrow streets. Different as this foreign journey seems to be from Jane Eyre's English pilgrimage, it suggests a similar point about women's disenfranchisement from culture. Also like Jane Eyre, Lucy represents all women who must struggle toward an integrated, mature, and independent identity by coming to terms with their need for love, and their dread of being single. So, like Jane, Lucy will confront the necessity of breaking through the debilitating roles available to the single women the Victorians termed "redundant."

It is ironic then that Harriet Martineau criticized *Villette* on the grounds that the characters think of nothing but love,[11] for that is precisely Brontë's point. Onboard *The Vivid*, Lucy is confronted with several women who are caught in this central female dilemma—a bride (with a husband who looks like an oil barrel) whose laughter, Lucy decides, must be the frenzy of despair; Ginevra Fanshawe, a frivolous schoolgirl on her way to Villette, who explains that she is one of five sisters who must marry elderly gentlemen with cash; and one Charlotte, the subject of the stewardess's letter, who seems to be on the brink of perpetrating an imprudent match. Although marriage seems no less painful a submission than a life of lonely isolation, Lucy exults on deck, thinking, "Stone walls do not a prison make, / Nor iron bars—a cage."[12] Yet, as always, her moment of triumph is immediately undercut. She too gets ill and must go below like the rest, and the verse remains ambiguous, since the mind which can liberate the caged prisoner can also provide walls and bars for those who are physically free.

On her arrival in Labassecour, Lucy is stripped of even the few objects and attributes she possesses. Her keys, her trunk, her money, and her language are equally useless. A stranger in a strange land, she becomes aware that her physical situation reflects her psychic state. With no destination in mind, she catches "at cobwebs," specifically at Ginevra's comment that her schoolmistress wants an English governess. "Accidentally" finding Madame Beck's establishment, she waits inside the salon with her eyes fixed on "a great white folding-door, with gilt mouldings" (chap. 7). It remains closed, but a voice at her elbow unexpectedly begins a symbolic questioning, so that Lucy must assure herself and her reader that "No ghost stood beside me, nor anything of spectral aspect" (chap. 7). But this is not entirely true. The landscape of her passage, as well as its fortuitous end, makes it seem as if Lucy has entered an enchanted dreamland filled with symbolically appropriate details, ruled by extremely improbable coincidences, and peopled by ghosts.

Recent critics of *Villette* frequently ignore these curiosities, focusing instead on the imagery, as if embarrassed by what they consider inferior or melodramatic plotting.[13] But as intelligent a reader as George Eliot found the novel's power "preternatural" and majestically testified to her fascination with *Villette* "which we, at least, would rather read for the third time than most new novels for the first." Eliot found the novel such a compelling structure for the riskiness of personal growth that she called her elopement with the already married George Henry Lewes a trip to "Labassecour."[14]

What makes the narrative seem authentically "preternatural" or uncanny is Brontë's representation of the psychic life of Lucy Snowe through a series of seemingly independent characters, as well as her use of contiguous events to dramatize and mythologize her imagery by demonstrating its psychosexual meaning. "When We Dead Awaken," Adrienne Rich explains, "everything outside our skins is an image/of this affliction."[15] And as Lucy fitfully awakens from her self-imposed living death, she resembles all those heroines, from the Grimms' Snow White to Kate Chopin's Edna Pontellier, whose awakenings are dangerous precisely because they might very well sense, as Rich does, that "never have we been closer to the truth/of the lies we were living." In other words, Lucy accidentally finds her way to Madame Beck's house because it is the house of her own self. And Madame Beck, who startles her visitor by entering magically through an invisible door, can effectively spy on Lucy because she is one of the many voices inhabiting and haunting Lucy's mind.

A woman whose eyes never "know the fire which is kindled in the heart or the softness which flows thence" (chap. 8), Madame Beck haunts the school in her soundless slippers and rules over all through espionage and surveillance. Lucy compares her with Minos, to Ignacia, to a prime minister, and a superintendent of police. She glides around spying at keyholes, oiling the doors, imprinting keys, opening drawers, carefully scrutinizing Lucy's private memorabilia, and turning the girl's pockets inside out. She is motivated only by self-interest, and so her face is a "face of stone" (chap. 8) and her aspect that of a man (chap. 8). For Madame Beck is a symbol of repression, the projection and embodiment of Lucy's commitment to self-control. Calm, self-contained, authoritative, she is alert to the dangerous passions that she must somehow control lest impropriety give her school a bad name. Her spying is therefore a form of voyeurism, and though it is deplored by Lucy, it is quickly clear that Lucy is simultaneously engaged in spying on Madame Beck. Like Lucy, Madame Beck dresses in decorous gray; like Lucy, she is attracted to the young Englishman Dr. John; and like Lucy, she is not his choice. In defeat, Madame Beck is capable of mastering herself. Not only does Lucy mimic Madame Beck's repressive tactics in the school room, she also applauds the way in which Madame Beck represses her desire for Dr. John: "Brava! once more, Madame Beck. I saw you matched against an Apollyon of a predilection: you fought a good fight, and you overcame!" (chap. 11). And in doing so, Lucy is applauding her own commitment to self-repression, her own impulse toward self-surveillance.

The success of Lucy's self-surveillance, however, is called into question by the number of activities that Madame Beck cannot control by means of *her* spying. Perhaps the most ironic of these involves her own daughter, a child appropriately named Desirée. A daemonic parody of Madame Beck, Desirée steals to the attic to open up the drawers and boxes of her *bonne*, which she tears to pieces; she secretly enters rooms in order to smash articles of porcelain or plunder preserves; she robs her mother and then buries the prize in a hole in the garden wall or in a cranny in the garret. Madame Beck's supervision has failed with Desirée, who is a sign that repression breeds revolt, and that revolt (when it comes) will itself involve secrecy, destruction, and deceit. That Lucy herself will rebel is further indicated by the story of the woman whose place she has come to fill, the nurserymaid called Madame "Svini." Actually an Irish Mrs. Sweeny, this alcoholic washerwoman has successfully passed herself off as an English lady in reduced circumstances by means of a splendid wardrobe that was clearly made for proportions other than her own. A counterfeiter, she reminds us that Lucy too hides her passions behind her costume. The split between restraint and indulgence, voyeurism and participation represented in the contrast between Lucy and Polly is repeated in the antagonism between Madame Beck on the one hand and Desirée, Madame Svini, and Ginevra Fanshawe on the other.

Carrying on two secret love affairs right under Madame's nose, it is Ginevra who best embodies Lucy's attraction to self-indulgence and freedom. The resemblance between Ginevra's satiric wit and Lucy's sardonic honesty provides the basis for Ginevra affectionately calling Lucy her "grandmother," "Timon," and "Diogenes." And Ginevra is aware, as no one else is, that Lucy is "a personage in disguise" (chap. 27). "But *are* you anybody?" (chap. 27) she repeatedly inquires of Lucy. It is Ginevra, too, with her familiar physical demonstrations, who violates Lucy's self-imposed isolation not only when she waltzes Lucy around, but also when she sits "gummed" to Lucy's side, obliging Lucy "sometimes to put an artful pin in my girdle by way of protection against her elbow" (chap. 28). For reasons that she never completely understands, Lucy shares her food with Ginevra, fantasizes about Ginevra's love life, and even admires Ginevra's flagrant narcissism. As their friendship develops, Lucy responds to this girl, who claims that she "*must* go out" (chap. 9) to the garden, where Lucy is actually mistaken for Ginevra.

What makes the garden especially valuable in Lucy's eyes is her knowledge that all else "is stone around, blank wall and hot pavement" (chap. 12). This "enclosed and planted spot of ground" is immediately associated with the illicit, with romantic passion, with every activity Madame Beck cannot control. It is the original Garden, a bit of nature within the city, a hiding place for Desirée's stolen goods, bordered by another establishment, a boy's school, from which rain down billets-doux intended for Ginevra but read by Lucy. When initially described, the garden is an emblem of the buried life:

... at the foot of ... a Methuselah of a peartree, dead, all but a few boughs which still faithfully renewed their perfumed snow in spring, and their honeysweet pendants in autumn—you saw, in scraping away the mossy earth between the half-bared roots, a glimpse of slab, smooth, hard, and black. The legend went, unconfirmed and unaccredited, but still propagated, that this was the portal of a vault, imprisoning deep beneath that ground, on whose surface grass grew and flowers bloomed, the bones of a girl whom a monkish conclave of the drear middle ages had here buried alive for some sin against her vow. [chap. 12]

Discovering what Catherine Morland had hoped to find, "some awful memorials of an injured and ill-fated nun" (*NA*, II, chap. 2), Lucy reads her own story in the nun's. However, unlike the convents that spawn erotic adventures in male literature from *Venus in the Cloister; or, the Nun in Her Smock* to Lewis's *The Monk*, the emblem of religious incarceration does not here provide privacy for a liberated sexuality.[16] On the contrary, both Lucy and the nun, when they align themselves with the monk's surveillance, cannot escape the confinement of chastity. Like the buried girl, Lucy haunts the forbidden alley because she is beginning to revolt against the constraints she originally countenanced. "Reason" and "imagination" are the terms she uses to describe the conflict between her conscious self-repression and the libidinal desires she fears and hopes will possess her, but significantly she maintains a sense of herself as separate from both forces and she therefore feels victimized by both.

Under a young crescent moon and some stars (which she remembers shining beside an old thorn in England), while sitting on the hidden seat of "l'allée défendue," Lucy experiences the dangerous feelings she has so long suppressed:

I had feelings: passive as I lived, little as I spoke, cold as I looked, when I thought of past days, I *could* feel. About the present, it was better to be stoical; about the future—such a future as mine—to be dead. And in catalepsy and a dead trance, I studiously held the quick of my nature. [chap. 12]

She recalls an earlier moment in the school dormitory when she was in a sense obliged to "live." During a storm, while the others began praying to their saints, Lucy crept outside the casement to sit on the ledge in the wet, wild, pitch dark, for "too resistless was the delight of staying with the wild hour, black and full of thunder, pealing out such an ode as language never delivered to man" (chap. 12). The English thorn, the experience of interiority in the garden, the ways in which that experience in tranquility recalls an earlier spot in time when Lucy felt the power of infinitude, all are reminiscent of the poetry of Wordsworth. So, too, are the diction, the negative syntax, the inverted word order. Unlike the poet, however, Lucy is not in the country but enclosed in a small park at the center of a city; she remembers herself in the wind, not swaying in the boughs of trees, but crouching on a window ledge. The ode she thought she heard was really terrible, not glorious. Like the nun and Lucy herself, the black and white sky was split and Lucy longed for an escape "upwards and onwards" (chap. 12). But like most of her desires, that longing had to be negated, this time because it was suicidal.

In personifying the wish for escape as Sisera, and the repression of it as Jael, Lucy explains how painful her self-division is. In the biblical story, Heber's wife, Jael, persuades the tired warrior to take rest in her tent, where she provides him with milk and a mantle. When Sisera sleeps, Jael takes a hammer and drives a nail through his temple, fastening him to the ground (Judges 4: 18–21). On the evening that Lucy remembers her own feelings, her Sisera is slumbering, for he has yet to experience the inevitable moment of horror still to come. But unlike the biblical victim, Lucy's Sisera never fully dies: her longings to escape imprisonment are but "transiently stunned, and at intervals would turn on the nail with a rebellious wrench: then did the temples bleed, and the brain thrill to its core" (chap. 12). The horror of her life, indeed, is the horror of repetition, specifically the periodic bleeding wound so feared by Frances Henri. For Lucy's existence is a living death because she is both the unconscious, dying stranger and the housekeeper who murders the unsuspecting guest. Both Polly and Lucy, both Ginevra and Madame Beck, Lucy is the nun who is immobilized by this internal conflict. No wonder she imagines herself as a snail, a fly caught in Madame Beck's cobwebs, or a spider flinging out its own precarious web. In the conflict within the house of Lucy's self, her antagonistic representatives testify to the fragmentation within that will eventually lead to her complete mental breakdown.

It is significant that all these women are linked, defined, and motivated by their common attraction to Dr. John. He is the bright-haired English missionary of Polly's book, the carrier of the burden of English healing arts, the powerful leopard with the golden mane, and Apollo the sun God, as well as the fearfully powerful lover whom Emily Dickinson was to call "the man of noon." Each woman woos Dr. John in her own way: Madame Beck hires him; Ginevra flirts with him; Lucy quietly helps him protect the woman he loves. In responding to Dr. John, Lucy aids Ginevra, frequents the garden, and experiences her own freedom. But, given the dialectic of her nature—the conflict between engagement with life and retreat from it—her amorous participation arouses the suspicions of Madame Beck, who opens up all her work boxes and investigates her locked drawers. Torn between what Ginevra and Madame Beck represent to her, Lucy experiences "soreness and laughter, and fire and grief" (chap. 13). She thinks she can resort to her usual remedies of self-restraint and repression; but, having experienced her own emotions, she finds that the casements and doors of the Rue Fossette open out into the summer garden and she acquires a new dress, a sign that she is tempted to participate in her own existence.

The principal sign of Lucy's desire to exist actively, however, is her role-playing in a school theatrical. She participates only after M. Paul commands her, "play you can: play you must" (chap. 14), and since she feels that there are no adequate roles provided for her, she finds her part particularly dreadful: she is assigned the role of an empty-headed fop who flirts to gain the hand of the fair coquette. Lucy fears that self-dramatization will expose her to ridicule, so her part is that of a fool; she fears that imaginative participation is immodest, so her part is masculine. Because she dreads participation, moreover, she must learn her role in the attic, where beetles, cobwebs, and rats cover cloaks said to conceal the nun.

By refusing to dress completely like a man onstage and by choosing only certain items to signify her male character, Lucy makes the role her own. But at the same time she is liberated by the male garments that she does select, and in this respect she reminds us of all those women artists who signal their artistic independence by disguising themselves as men or, more frequently, by engaging in a transvestite parody of symbols of masculine authority. Though cross-dressing can surely signal self-division, paradoxically it can also liberate women from self-hatred, allowing for the freer expression of love for other women. Certainly, dressed in a man's jacket onstage, Lucy actively woos the heroine, played by Ginevra. Unable to attract Dr. John herself, Lucy can stimulate some kind of response from him, even if only anger, by wooing and winning Ginevra. But she can simultaneously appreciate a girl who embodies her own potential gaiety. As if to show that this play-acting is an emblem for all role-playing, after her participation in the theatrical Lucy taunts Dr. John in the garden, in an attempt to deflate the sentimental fictions he has created about Ginevra. Naturally, however, the next morning she decides to "lock up" her relish for theatrical and social acting because "it would not do for a mere looker-on at life" (chap. 14).

Since, as we have seen, the events of the plot chart Lucy's internal drama, the crisis of the play (when Lucy comes out on the stage) can be said to cause the confinement and isolation she experiences during the long vacation when she is left alone in the school with a deformed cretin whose stepmother will not allow her to come home. Lucy feels as if she is imprisoned with some strange untamed animal, for the cretin is a last nightmarish version of herself—unwanted, lethargic, silent, warped in mind and body, slothful, indolent, and angry. Ironically, however, the cretin, luckier than her keeper, is finally taken away by an aunt. Entirely alone, Lucy is then haunted by Ginevra, who becomes her own heroine in a succession of intricately imagined fantasies. Her ensuing illness is her final, anguished recognition of her own life-in-death: she sees the white dormitory beds turned into spectres, "the coronal of each became a deaths-head, huge and sun-bleached—dead dreams of an earlier world and mightier race lay frozen in their wide gaping eyeholes" (chap. 15), and she feels that "Fate was of stone, and Hope a false idol—blind, bloodless, and of granite core" (chap. 15). Lucy is enfolded in a blank despair not far removed from Christina Rossetti's bleak "land with neither night nor day, / Nor heat nor cold, nor any wind nor rain, / Nor hills nor valleys."[17] Finally it is the insufferable thought of being no more loved, even by the dead, that drives Lucy out of the house which is "crushing as the slab of a tomb" (chap. 15).

But she can only escape one confining space for an even more limiting one, the confessional. Nothing is more irritating to some readers than the anti-Papist prejudice of *Villette*. But for Brontë, obsessively concerned with feelings of unreality and duplicity, Catholicism seems to represent the institutionalization of Lucy's internal schisms, permitting sensual indulgence by way of counterpoise to jealous spiritual restraint (chap. 14) and encouraging fervent zeal by means of surveillance or privation. "Tales that were nightmares of oppression, privation and agony" (chap. 13), the saints' lives, make Lucy's temples, heart, and wrist throb with excitement, so repellent are they to her, for she sees Catholicism as slavery. But precisely because Catholicism represents a sort of sanctioned schizophrenia, she finds herself attracted to it, and in her illness she kneels on the stone pavement in a Catholic church. Inhabiting the nun's walk, she has always lived hooded in gray to hide the zealot within (chap. 22). Now, seeking refuge within the confessional, she turns to this opening for community and communication which are as welcome to her "as bread to one in extremity of want" (chap. 15).

But she can only confess that she does not belong in this narrow space which cannot contain her: "mon père, je suis Protestante" (chap. 15). Using the only language at her disposal, a foreign language that persistently feels strange on her lips, Lucy has to experience her nonconformity, her Protestantism, as a sin, the sign of her rejection of any authority that denies her the right to be, whether that authority originates inside or outside herself. The "father" claims that for some there is only "bread of affliction and waters of affliction" (chap. 15), and his counsel reminds us that Brontë's virulent anti-Catholicism is informed by her strong attack on the masculine domination that pervades all forms of Christianity from its myths of origin to its social institutions. Although Lucy is grateful for the kindness of the priest, she would no more contemplate coming near him again than she would think of "walking into a Babylonish furnace." The mercy of the Virgin Mother may make the church seem maternal, as Nina Auerbach has recently argued,[18] but only momentarily for Lucy. She realizes that the priest wants to "kindle, blow and stir up" zeal that would mean she might "instead of writing this heretic narrative, be counting [her] beads in the cell of a certain Carmelite convent." Indeed Lucy will become increasingly certain, as she proceeds to tell her story, that nuns do fret at their convent walls, and that the church is a patriarchal structure with the power to imprison her.

Because she has nowhere else to go, after leaving the confessional she is "immeshed in a network of turns unknown" in the narrow, wind-blown streets. Battered by the storm and pitched "headlong down an abyss," she recalls the fallen angel himself and that poor orphan child sent so far and so lonely, with no sense of her own mission or destiny. While Wordsworth's Lucy experiences the protection of nature—"an overseeing power / To kindle or restrain"—Brontë's Lucy is caught in the horror of her own private dialectic. While Wordsworth's Lucy sports gleefully like a fawn across the lawn, even as she is blessed with the balm of "the silence and the calm/Of mute insensate things," Brontë's Lucy—because she lives unknown, among untrodden ways—is condemned to a wind-beaten expulsion into nowhere or a suffocating burial in her own non-existence.

* * *

It is amazing, however, how mysterious Lucy's complaint remains. Indeed, unless one interprets backwards from the breakdown, it is almost incomprehensible: Lucy's conflicts are hidden because, as we have seen, she represents them through the activity of other people. As self-effacing a narrator as she is a character, she often seems to be telling any story but her own. Polly Home, Miss Marchmont, Madame Beck, and Ginevra are each presented in more detail, with more analysis, than Lucy herself. The resulting obscurity means that generations of readers have assumed Brontë did not realize her subject until she was half-finished with the book. It means, too, that the work's mythic elements, although recognized, have been generally misunderstood or rejected as unjustifiable. And, after all, why should Lucy's schizophrenia be viewed as a generic problem facing all women? It is this question, with all that it implies, that Brontë confronts in the interlude at the center of *Villette*.

We have already seen that, in telling the stories of other women, Lucy is telling her own tale with as much evasion and revelation as Brontë is in recounting her personal experiences through the history of Lucy Snowe. Just as Brontë alters her past in order to reveal it, Lucy's ambivalence about her "heretic narrative" (chap. 15) causes her to leave much unsaid. Certainly there is a notable lack of specificity in her account. The terrors of her childhood, the loss of her parents, the unreturned love she feels for Dr. John, and the dread of her nightmares during the long vacation are recounted in a curiously allusive way. Instead of describing the actual events, for instance, Lucy frequently uses water imagery to express her feelings of anguish at these moments of suffering. Her turbulent childhood is a time of briny waves when finally "the ship was lost, the crew perished" (chap. 4); Dr. John's indifference makes her feel like "the rock struck, and Meribah's waters gushing out" (chap. 13); during the long vacation, she sickens because of tempestuous and wet weather bringing a dream that forces to her lips a black, strong, strange drink drawn from the boundless sea (chap. 15). This imagery is especially difficult because water is simultaneously associated with security. For example, Lucy remembers her visits to the Brettons as peaceful intervals, like "the sojourn of Christian and Hopeful beside a certain pleasant stream" (chap. 1). This last life-giving aspect of water is nowhere more apparent than in Lucy's return to consciousness after her headlong pitch down the abyss. At this point she discovers herself in the Bretton home, now miraculously placed just outside the city of Villette. Waking in the blue-green room of La Terrasse, she feels reborn into the comfort of a deep submarine chamber. When she has reached this safe asylum (complete with wonderful tea, seedcake, and godmother), she can only pray to be content with a temperate draught of the living stream.

Although she is now willing to drink, however, she continues to fear that once she succumbs to her thirst she will apply too passionately to the welcome waters. Nevertheless, Lucy is given a second chance: she is reborn into the same conflict, but with the realization that she cannot allow herself to die of thirst. As in her earlier novels, Brontë traces the woman's revolt against paternalism in her heroine's ambivalence about God the Father. Jane Eyre faced the overwhelming "currents" of St. John *Rivers'* enthusiasm which threatened to destroy her as much as the total absence of faith implied by the unredemptive role of *Grace/Poole*. In *Villette*, Lucy Snowe wants to believe that "the waiting waters will stir for the cripple and the blind, the dumb and the possessed" who "will be led to bathe" (chap. 17). Yet, she knows that "Thousands lie round the pool, weeping and despairing, to see it through slow years, stagnant" (chap. 17). If the waters stir, what do they bring? Do the weeping and despairing wait for death or resurrection? Drowning or baptism? Immersion or engulfment? Lucy never departs from the subjunctive or imperative or interrogative when discussing the redemption to come, because her desire for such salvation is always expressed as a hope and a prayer, never as a belief. Aware that life on earth is based on an inequality, which has presumably been countenanced by a power greater than herself, she sardonically, almost sarcastically, admits that His will shall be done, "whether we humble ourselves to resignation or not" (chap. 38).

The very problematic quality of the water imagery, then, reflects Lucy's ambivalence. It is as confusing as it is illuminating, as much a camouflage as a disclosure. Her fear of role-playing quite understandably qualifies the way she speaks or writes, and her reticence as a narrator makes her especially unreliable when she deals with what she most fears. To the consternation of many critics who have bemoaned her trickery,[19] not only does she withhold Dr. John's last name from the reader, she never divulges the contents of his letters, and, until the end of her story, she persistently disclaims warm feelings for him. Furthermore, she consistently withholds information from other characters out of mere perversity. She never, for instance, voluntarily tells Dr. John that he helped her on the night of her arrival in Villette, or that she remembers him as Graham from Bretton days; later, when she recounts an evening at a concert to Ginevra, she falsifies the account; and even when she wishes to tell M. Paul that she has heard his story, she mockingly reverses what she has learned. Indeed, although Lucy is silent in many scenes, when she does speak out, her voice retreats from the perils of self-definition behind sarcasm and irony. "But if I feel, may I *never* express?" she asks herself, only to hear her reason declare, "Never!" (chap. 21). Even in the garden, she can only parody Ginevra and Dr. John (chaps. 14–15), and when her meaning is misunderstood on any of these occasions, she takes "pleasure in thinking of the contrast between reality and [her] description" (chap. 21).

Why would Brontë choose a narrator who purposefully tries to evade the issues or mislead the reader? This is what Lucy seems to do when she allows the reader to picture her childhood "as a bark slumbering through halcyon weather" because "A great many women and girls are supposed to pass their lives something in this fashion" (chap. 4). Why does Brontë choose a voyeur to narrate a fictional biography when this means that the narrator insists on telling the tale as if some other, more attractive woman were its central character? Obviously, Lucy's life, her sense of herself, does not conform to the literary or social stereotypes provided by her culture to define and circumscribe female life. Resembling Goethe's Makarie in that she too feels as if she has no story, Lucy cannot employ the narrative structures available to her, yet there are no existing alternatives. So she finds herself using and abusing—presenting and undercutting—images and stories of male devising, even as she omits or elides what has been deemed unsuitable, improper, or aberrant in her own experience.

That Lucy feels anxious and guilty about her narrative is evident when she wonders whether an account of her misfortunes might not merely disturb others, whether the half-drowned life-boatman shouldn't keep his own counsel and spin no yarns (chap. 17). At more than one point in her life, she considers it wise, for those who have experienced inner turmoil or madness in solitary confinement, to keep quiet (chap. 24). Resulting sometimes in guilty acquiescence and sometimes in angry revolt, the disparity between what is publicly expected of her and her private sense of herself becomes the source of Lucy's feelings of unreality. Not the little girl lost (Polly), or the coquette (Ginevra), or the male manqué (Madame Beck), or the buried nun (in the garden), Lucy cannot be contained by the roles available to her. But neither is she free of them, since all these women do represent aspects of herself. Significantly, however, none of these roles ascribe to women the initiative, the intelligence, or the need to tell their own stories. Thus, Lucy's evasions as a narrator indicate how far she (and all women) have come from silent submission and also how far all must yet go in finding a voice. In struggling against the confining forms she inherits, Lucy is truly involved in a mythic undertaking—an attempt to create an adequate fiction of her own. *Villette* is a novel that falls into two almost equally divided sections: the first part takes Lucy up to the episode of the confessional, and the second recounts her renewed attempt to make her own way in Madame Beck's establishment; but in the interlude at the Brettons' Brontë explores why and how the aesthetic conventions of patriarchal culture are as imprisoning for women as sexist economic, social, and political institutions.

As in her other novels, Brontë charts a course of imprisonment, escape, and exclusion until the heroine, near death from starvation, fortuitously discovers a family of her own. That Lucy has found some degree of self-knowledge through her illness is represented by her coincidental reunion with the Brettons. That she is in some ways healed is made apparent through her quarrel with Dr. John Graham Bretton. Lucy refuses to submit to his view of Ginevra as a goddess, and after calling him a slave, she manages only to agree to differ with him. She sees him as a worshipper ready with the votive offering at the shrine of his favorite saint (chap. 18). In making this charge, she calls attention to the ways in which romantic love (like the spiritual love promulgated by the Catholic church) depends on coercion and slavery—on a loss of independence, freedom, and self-respect for both the worshipper and the one worshipped.

Chapter 19, "The Cleopatra," is crucial in elaborating this point. When Dr. John takes Lucy sight-seeing to a museum, she is struck by the lounging self-importance of the painted heroine of stage and story. To slender Lucy, the huge Egyptian queen looks as absurdly inflated as the manner of her presentation: the enormous canvas is cordoned off, fronted by a cushioned bench for the adoring public. Lucy and her creator are plainly aware of the absurdity of such art, and Lucy has to struggle against the approbation which the monster painting seems to demand as its right. She refuses to treat the portrait as an autonomous entity, separate from reality, just as she defies the rhetoric of the religious paintings of "La vie d'une femme" that M. Paul commends to her attention. The exemplary women in these portraits are "Bloodless, brainless nonentities!" she exclaims, as vapid, interestingly, as "ghosts," because they have nothing to do with life as Lucy knows it. Their piety and patience as young lady, wife, mother, and widow leave her as cold as Cleopatra's voluptuous sensuality.

Of course the paintings are meant to examine the ridiculous roles men assign women, and thus the chapter is arranged to maximize the reader's consciousness of how varying male responses to female images are uniformly produced by the male pride that seeks to control women. In squeamish Dr. John, who deposits and collects Lucy; voyeuristic M. Paul, who turns her away from Cleopatra while himself finding her "Une femme superbe"; and foppish de Hamal, who minces daintily in front of the painting, Brontë describes the range of male responses to the completely sexual Cleopatra and the completely desexed, exemplary girl-wife-mother-widow, as Kate Millett has shown.[20]

In particular, because they parody Lucy's inner conflict between assertive sensuality and ascetic submission, the Cleopatra and "La vie d'une femme" perpetrate the fallacy that one of these extremes can—or should— become an identity. Significantly, the rhetoric of the paintings and of the museum in which they are displayed is commercial, propagandistic, and complacent: the paintings are valuable possessions, each with a message, each presented as a finished and admirable object. Just as commercial are the bourgeois arts at the concert Lucy attends with Dr. John and his mother. Interestingly, it is here that Dr. John decides that Ginevra Fanshawe is not even a pure-minded woman, much less a pure angel. But it is not simply his squeamishness about female sexuality that is illuminated on this occasion, for the very opulence of the concert hall testifies to the smugness of the arts practiced there and the materialism of the people present.

Lucy's imagination, however, is touched by neither the paintings at the museum nor the performances at the civic concert because she resents the manipulation she associates with their magic. These arts are not ennobling because they seem egotistical, coercive, not unlike the grand processions "of the church and the army—priests with relics, and soldiers with weapons" (chap. 36). In fact, declares Lucy, the Catholic church uses its theatrical ceremonies so that "a Priesthood"—an apt emblem of patriarchy—"might march straight on and straight upward to an all-dominating eminence" (chap. 36). Nevertheless, at the concert the illusions perpetrated by the architecture are successfully deceptive: everyone except Lucy seems unaware that the Queen is involved in a tragic drama with her husband, who is possessed by the same ghost that haunts Lucy, "the spectre, Hypochrondria" (chap. 20). The social and aesthetic conventions of the concert appear to cast a spell over the people, who are blinded to the King's actual state by the illusion of state pomp. The arts of the concert, like those of the museum and the church, perpetuate false myths that insure the continuance of patriarchal forms, both secular and sacred, that are themselves devoid of intrinsic power or morality.

Although Dr. John takes Lucy to see the actress Vashti only after she has left La Terrasse for the Rue Fossette, this dramatic performance is a fitting conclusion to Lucy's aesthetic excursions. Once again, the audience is the elite of Villette society. But this time Lucy's imagination is touched and she experiences the tremendous power of the artist: "in the uttermost frenzy of energy is each maenad movement royally, imperially, incedingly upborne" (chap. 23). Certainly Lucy's description of Vashti is so fervently rhapsodic as to be almost incoherent. But most simply Vashti is a player of parts whose acting is destroying her. Therefore, as many critics have noted, "this woman termed 'plain'" (chap. 23) is a monitory image for Lucy, justifying her own reticence.[21] Indeed, at least one woman poet was drawn to Vashti because of this biblical queen's determination not to perform. The Black American poet Frances Harper wrote of a "Vashti" who declares "I never will be seen,"[22] and Brontë's Vashti illuminates the impetus behind such a vow by demonstrating the annihilating power of the libidinal energies unleashed by artistic performance. Throughout the novel, Lucy has pleaded guiltless "of that curse, an over-heated and discursive imagination" (chap. 2). But although she has tried to strike a bargain between the two sides of herself, buying an internal life of thought nourished by the "necromantic joys" (chap. 8) of fancy at the high price of an external life limited to drudgery, the imaginative power cannot, Brontë shows, be contained in this way: it resurrects all those feelings that Lucy thought she had so ably put to death. During her mental breakdown, as we saw, her imagination recalled the dead in nightmares, roused the ghosts that haunted her, and transformed the dormitory into a replica of her own mind, a chamber of horrors.

Is the magic of art seen as necromantic for women because it revitalizes females deadened by male myths? After she has returned to Madame Beck's, Lucy finds the release offered by the imagination quite tempting. Reason, the cruel teacher at the front of the room, is associated with frigid beds and barren board; but imagination is the winged angel that appeases with sweet foods and warmth. A daughter of heaven, imagination is the goddess from whom Lucy seeks solace:

> Temples have been reared to the Sun—altars dedicated to the Moon. Oh, greater glory! To thee neither hands build, nor lips consecrecrate: but hearts, through ages, are faithful to thy worship. *A dwelling thou hast, too wide for walls, too high for dome— a temple whose floors are space*—rites whose mysteries transpire in presence, to the kindling, the harmony of worlds! [chap. 21; italics ours]

Neither the male sun nor the female moon compare with this androgynous, imaginative power which cannot be contained or confined. But even as she praises the freedom, the expansiveness, of a force that transcends all limits, Lucy fears that, for her, the power-that-cannot-be-housed is never to be attained except in the dying dreams of an exile.

Beyond its representation of Lucy's subjective drama, the Vashti performance is also an important statement about the dangers of the imagination for all women. Vashti's passionate acting causes her to be rejected by proper society. Dr. John, for instance, "judged her as a woman, not an artist: it was a branding judgment" (chap. 23). But more profoundly important than his societal rejection is Vashti's own sense of being damned: "Fallen, insurgent, banished, she remembers the heaven where she rebelled. Heaven's light, following her exile, pierces its confines, and discloses their forlorn remoteness" (chap. 23). Lucy had at first thought the presence on stage "was only a woman." But she "found upon her something neither of woman nor of man: in each of her eyes sat a devil." These evil forces wrote "HELL" on her brow. They also "cried sore and rent the tenement they haunted, but still refused to be exorcised." The incarnation of "Hate and Murder and Madness" (chap. 23), Vashti is the familiar figure we saw in *Frankenstein* and in *Wuthering Heights*, the Satanic Eve whose artistry of death is a testimonial to her fall from grace and her revolt against the tyranny of heaven as well as her revenge against the fall and the exile she reenacts with each performance onstage.

Having experienced the origin of her own passions, Vashti will be punished for a rebellion that is decidedly futile for women. Certainly this is what Racine implies in *Phèdre*, which is the most famous and passionate role played by Vashti's historical prototype, the great French tragedienne Rachel.[23] But the violence of Vashti's acting—she stands onstage "locked in struggle, rigid in resistance"—suggests that she is actually struggling against the fate of the character she plays, much as Lucy struggles against the uncongenial roles she plays. Vashti's resistance to "the rape of every faculty" represents the plight of the female artist who tries to subvert the lessons of female submission implied—if not asserted—by art that damns the heroine's sexuality as the source of chaos and suffering. Because Vashti is portrayed as an uncontainable woman, her power will release a passion that engulfs not only the spectator but Vashti herself as well.

Twice Lucy interrupts her rhapsodic description of this actress to indicate that Vashti puts to shame the artist of the Cleopatra. Unlike the false artists who abound in *Villette*, Vashti uses her art not to manipulate others, but to represent herself. Her art, in other words, is confessional, unfinished—not a product, but an act; not an object meant to contain or coerce, but a personal utterance. Indeed, it is even a kind of strip show, a form of the female suicidal self-exposure that pornographers from Sade to the nameless producers of snuff films have exploited, so that her costly self-display recalls the pained ironic cry of Plath's "Lady Lazarus": "I turn and burn, / Do not think I underestimate your great concern."[24] At the same time, Vashti's performance also inevitably reminds us of the dance of death the Queen must do in her fiery shoes at the end of "Snow White." But while Brontë presents Vashti's suffering, she also emphasizes that this art is a feminist reaction to patriarchal aesthetics, and so Lucy withholds the "real" name of the actress and calls her, instead, "Vashti."

Unlike the queen of Villette, who seeks to solace her lord, or the queen of the Nile, who seems made for male pleasure, Queen Vashti of the Book of Esther refuses to placate King Ahasuerus. Quite gratuitously it seems, on the seventh day, when all patriarchs rest, the king calls on Vashti to display her beauty before the princes of the realm, and she refuses to come. Her revolt makes the princes fear that their wives will be filled with contempt for them. Brontë's actress, like the biblical queen, refuses to be treated as an object, and consciously rejects art that dehumanizes its subject or its audience. By transcending the distinctions between private and public, between person and artist, between artist and art, Vashti calls into question, therefore, the closed forms of male culture. Like that of the biblical queen, her protest means the loss of her estate, banishment from the king's sight. And like sinister Lady Lazarus, who ominously warns that "there is a charge, a very large charge, / For a word or a touch," Vashti puts on an inflammatory performance which so subverts the social order that it actually seems to set the theater on fire and sends all the wealthy patrons rushing outside to save their lives. Even as her drama proposes an alternative to patriarchal culture, then, it defines the pain of female artistry, and the revengeful power of female rebellion.

* * *

On a dark, rainy night recalling that similar night "not a year ago" (chap. 20), Lucy arrives for the second time at Madame Beck's and immediately enters into the old conflict—with if anything, greater intensity. Haunted by her desire for a letter from Dr. John, describing it—when it comes—as "nourishing and salubrious meat," she places it unopened into a locked case, within a closed drawer, inside the locked dormitory, within the school. Just as she had previously hidden behind masks and fantastic roles, she now experiences emotions which are represented once again by the bleak, black, cold garret where she reads these concealed letters. In this "dungeon under the leads" (chap. 22), she experiences "a sort of gliding out from the direction of the black recess haunted by the malefactor cloaks" (chap. 22). Once again in Brontë's fiction, the madwoman in the attic emerges as a projection of her heroine's secret desires, in this case Lucy's need for nullity.

As Charles Burkhart explains in *Charlotte Brontë: A Psychosexual Study of Her Novels*, and as both E. D. H. Johnson and Robert Heilman note in perceptive articles, the nun appears to Lucy on five separate occasions, at moments of great passion, when she is an actor in her own life.[25] The apparition embodies her anxiety not only about the imagination and passion, but about her very right to exist. Like Sylvia Plath, who feels her own emptiness "echo[ing] to the least footfall," Lucy is "Nun-hearted and blind to the world."[26] Dr. John is correct, then, in assuming that the nun comes out of Lucy's diseased brain: Lucy has already played the role of de Hamal on the stage, and now *he* is playing her role as the nun in Madame Beck's house. But this psychoanalytic interpretation is limited, as Lucy herself notes.

For one thing, Lucy is haunted by an image that has both attracted and repelled many women before her. Told often enough that they are the source of sin, women may well begin feeling guilty as they accept the necessity for penance. Taught effectively enough that they are irrelevant to the important processes of society, women begin to feel they are living invisibly. Thus the nun is not only a projection of Lucy's desire to submit in silence, to accept confinement, to dress in shadowy black, to conceal her face, to desexualize herself; the nun's way is also symbolic for Lucy of the only socially acceptable life available to single women—a life of service, self-abnegation, and chastity.[27] Her fascinated dread of the nun corresponds, then, to Margaret Fuller's rage at seeing a girl take the veil, a ceremony in which the black-robed sisters look "like crows or ravens at their ominous feasts." A contemporary of Brontë's and an exile, she too is convinced that where the nun's captivity is "enforced or repented of, no hell would be worse."[28]

Yet Lucy's nun is no longer buried. If she is the nun of legend, she haunts the garret, according to the story, as a protest against male injustice. Her refusal to remain buried suggests, therefore, that Lucy may very well be moving toward some kind of rejection of her own conventlike life-in-death. If, unlike condescending Dr. John, we take seriously Lucy's puzzlement over her vision in the garret, we realize that she has become enmeshed in a mystery no less baffling than those faced by Jane Eyre and Caroline Helstone: as a single woman, how can she escape the nun's fate? Haunted by her avatars, Lucy Snowe becomes a detective following clues to piece out an identity, for here, as in *Jane Eyre*, Brontë joins the *Bildungsroman* to the mystery story to demonstrate that growing up female requires vigilant demystification of an enigmatic, male-dominated world.

In this connection it is notable that, in some mysterious way, out of the ice of the garret nun and the fire of Vashti a figure now emerges who is able to combine fire and ice, instead of being split apart by these elements as Lucy is. Polly's "coincidental" appearance at this point in the plot draws our attention to the impossibility of Lucy ever finding a solution through Dr. John. Much as Lucy was reborn at La Terrasse, Polly is born again in the theater: Dr. John opens the dense mass of the crowd, boring through a flesh-and-blood rock—solid, hot, and suffocating—until he and Lucy are brought out into the freezing night and then Polly appears, light as a child (chap. 23). A vital and vestal flame, surrounded by gentle "hoar-frost" (chap. 32), self-contained yet loving, delicate yet strong, Polly remembers the old Bretton days as well as Lucy, and she also receives Dr. John's letters with excitement, carrying them upstairs to secure the treasures under lock and key before savoring them at her leisure. She is, in fact, Lucy Snowe born under a lucky star, and her emergence marks the end of Dr. John's consciousness of Lucy herself as anything but an inoffensive shadow.

When Dr. John's letters to her cease—as cease they now must—Lucy is once again obsessed with images of confinement and starvation. Feeling like a hermit stagnant in his cell, she tries to convince herself that the wise solitary would lock up his own emotions and submit to his snow sepulcher in the hope of a spring thaw. But she knows that the frost might very well "get into his heart" (chap. 24), and for seven weeks, as she awaits a letter, she feels just like a caged and starving animal awaiting food. Reliving the horrors of the long vacation, she finally drops the "tone of false calm which, long to sustain, outwears nature's endurance" (chap. 24), and decides to "Call anguish—anguish, and despair—despair" (chap. 31). In the process of writing her life history, we realize, Lucy has continued the learning process begun by the events she narrates, and the change in her outlook is reflected perhaps most specifically in the way she tells the story of the growing love between Dr. John and Polly.

Painfully, honestly, Lucy tells the story of her rejection of romance. This rejection is forced upon Lucy because, as she says, "the goodly river is bending to another course" (chap. 26). Her response is characteristic: she buries Dr. John's letters in a hermetically sealed jar, in a hole at the base of the pear tree, which she then covers over with slate. The episode, Brontë implies, suggests that worship of the godly male, desire for romantic love and male protection, is so deeply bred into Lucy that, at this point, she can only try to repress it. But the necromantic power of the imagination renders this kind of burial inadequate, and the appearance of the nun at the burial site forecasts the ways in which Dr. John will continue to haunt Lucy: feeling the tomb unquiet she will dream "Strangely of disturbed earth," and (in a strange pre-vision of the story of Lizzie Siddal Rossetti) of hair, "still golden, and living, obtruded through coffin-chinks" (chap. 31). But the burial does allow her to endure, to befriend Polly, to speak with self-possession to Dr. John—refusing to be used by him as an "officious soubrette in a love drama" (chap. 27)—and to be reserved when she is hurt by M. Paul.

Excluded from romance, Lucy discovers that romantic love is itself no panacea. Polly had criticized Schiller's ballad "Das Mädchens Klage" because the summit of earthly happiness is not to love, but to be loved (chap. 26). But Lucy begins to understand that neither loving nor being loved insure against egotism, against, for instance, the insensitivity of Polly's recital of the Schiller poem, which sentimentalizes precisely the suffering Lucy has experienced. Ultimately, it is the recognition of her own self, newly emerged in Polly, that frees Lucy from feeling that she is a nun (none) as a single woman. A delicate dame, a fairy thing, an exquisite imp, a childish sprite who still lisps, a faun, a lamb, and finally a pet puppy, Polly is the paragon of romance—the perfect lady—and Lucy's metaphors demonstrate that she has begun to understand the limits of a role that allows Polly to remain less than an adult. She sees as well the selfishness of Dr. John, who is equally thoughtless, not even realizing, for example, that he has forgotten Lucy's very existence for months, despite his ostensible concern about her hypochrondria. There is, Lucy discovers, "a certain infatuation of egotism" (chap. 37) in lovers, which hurts not only their friends but themselves, for even Polly must be careful to preserve her chaste frost, or she will lose the worship of the fastidious doctor. Finally, there is something malevolent about the amulet Polly makes, the spell to bind her men, since she plaits together her father's gray lock and the golden hairs of Dr. John to prison them in a locket laid at her heart, an object all too reminiscent of Lucy's buried cache (chap. 37).

As if to emphasize the false expectations created by romantic enthrallment, Brontë has Lucy set the glamour of the "romantic" courtship against her own growing friendship with M. Paul, who is emphatically an anti-hero—small, dark, middle-aged, tyrannical, self-indulgent, sometimes cruel, even at times a fool. His very faults, however, make it impossible for Lucy to see him as anything other than an equal. Their relationship, we soon realize, is combative because they are equals, because they are so much alike. Paul, in fact, recognizes Lucy's capacity for passion because of his own fiery nature, and he is convinced that their foreheads, their eyes, even certain tones of voice are similar. They share love of liberty, hatred of injustice, enjoyment of the "allée défendue" in the garden. Paul also, we discover, had a passion that "died in the past—in the present it lies buried—its grave is deep-dug, well-heaped, and many winters old" (chap. 29). Consequently, he too has allowed himself to become a voyeur, peeking through a magic lattice into the garden to spy upon the unwitting inhabitants. For both Paul and Lucy are tainted by the manipulative, repressive ways in which they have managed to lead a buried life, and so both are haunted by the nun, who finally visits them when they stand together under the trees. Together they begin to participate in the joys of food, of story-telling, of walks in the country, of flowered hats and brightly colored clothes. But their relationship is constantly impeded by the haunting which the nun represents and by their common fears of human contact.

The inequality of their relationship, moreover, is dramatized when M. Paul becomes Lucy's teacher, for Paul Carl David Emmanuel only encourages his pupil when her intellectual efforts are marked by "preternatural imbecility." Cruel when she seems to surpass "the limits proper to [her] sex," he causes Lucy to feel the stir of ambition: "Whatever my powers—feminine or the contrary—God had given them, and I felt resolute to be ashamed of no faculty of His bestowal" (chap. 30). Significantly, Paul persists in believing that, "as monkeys are said to have the power of speech if they would but use it" (chap. 30), Lucy is criminally concealing a knowledge of both Greek and Latin. He is convinced that she must be "a sort of 'lusus naturae,'" a monstrous accident, for "he believed in his soul that lovely, placid, and passive feminine mediocrity was the only pillow on which manly thought and sense could find rest for its aching temples" (chap. 30).

Paul, in short, wants Lucy to join the ranks of Milton's dutiful daughters by executing his commands either as a secretary who transcribes his performances or as a writer who will improvise in French on prescribed subjects. Naturally she is horrified at the idea of becoming his creature and writing "for a show and to order, perched up on a platform," in part because she is convinced that "the Creative Impulse," which she imagines as a male muse and the "most maddening of masters," would stand "all cold, all indurated, all granite, a dark Baal with carven lips and blank eye-balls, and breast like the stone face of a tomb" (chap. 30). When, in spite of her remonstrances, she is finally compelled by Paul to submit to an examination, she discovers that his professorial colleagues are the same two men whose lecherous pursuit in the dark streets of Villette had so terrified her on her arrival. This satiric perspective on respectable society liberates her sufficiently so she can express her disdain for M. Paul's petty tyrannies by producing a scathing portrait of "a red, random beldame with arms akimbo" who represents that capriciously powerful bitch goddess, "Human Nature" (chap. 26).

* * *

It is interesting, in this regard, that the critics of *Villette* have uniformly ignored one of the most curious episodes of the novel, one which reflects the great anxiety that emerging love produces in Lucy. In the chapter entitled "Malevola," Lucy resembles the typical fairy-tale little girl who must carry a basket of fruit to her grandmother's house. Madame Beck gives her a basket to deliver to Madame Walravens on the occasion of her birthday. In spite of a heavy rain that begins as soon as she enters the old *Basse-Ville* to reach the Rue des *Mages*, in spite of the hostile servant at the door, Lucy manages to enter the old house. In the salon, she stares at a picture that magically rolls back, revealing an arched passageway, a mystic winding stair of cold stone and a most curious figure:

> She might be three feet high, but she had no shape; her skinny hands rested upon each other, and pressed the gold knob of a wand-like ivory staff. Her face was large, set, not upon her shoulders, but before her breast; she seemed to have no neck; I should have said there were a hundred years in her features, and more perhaps in her eyes—her malign, unfriendly eyes, with thick grey brows above, and livid lids all round. How severely they viewed me, with a sort of dull displeasure! [chap. 34]

Madame Walravens curses Madame Beck's felicitations; when she turns to go, a peal of thunder breaks out. Her home seems an "enchanted castle," the storm a "spell-wakened tempest" (chap. 34). Finally she vanishes as mysteriously as she appeared. Her very name illustrates her ancestry: we have already seen that walls are associated repeatedly with imprisonment, while the raven is a traditional Celtic image of the hag who destroys children. And Madame Walravens *has*, we learn, destroyed a child by confining her: Lucy is told that she caused the death of her grandchild, Justine Marie, by opposing her match with the poverty-striken M. Paul, thereby causing the girl to withdraw into a convent where she had died twenty years ago. With her deformed body, her great age, her malignant look, and her staff, Madame Walravens is clearly a witch.

In fact, coming downstairs from the top of the house, Madame Walravens is yet another vindictive madwoman of the attic, and, like Bertha Mason Rochester, she is malevolently enraged, "with all the violence of a temper which deformity made sometimes daemonic" (chap. 34). Having outlived her husband, her son, and her son's child, she seems especially maddened against those on the brink of matrimonial happiness. Thus, as the terrible mother who seeks to take revenge, she enacts at the end of *Villette* a role which seems to be a final (and most intense) image of Lucy's repressed anger at the injustice of men and male culture, for in journeying to this ancient house in the oldest part of the city, Lucy has met her darkest and most secret avatar. It seems likely, indeed, that it is Lucy's unconscious and unspeakable will that Madame Walravens enacts when she sends Paul on a typically witchy quest for treasure in (of all places) *Basse/terre*. Since, as Anne Ross shows, the hag-raven goddess survives in the folklore of howling *banshees* who wail when death approaches,[29] it seems significant that, as Lucy confesses, she has always feared the gasping, tormented east wind, source of the legend of the Banshee (chap. 4). Furthermore, waiting for Paul to return to her, Lucy—praying, "Peace, Peace, Banshee"—cannot lull the destructive blast of the wind on the stormy sea (chap. 42). Finding M. Paul "more [her] own" after his death, Lucy understandably concludes her narrative with a reference to Madame Walravens's long life.

But if Madame Walravens is the madwoman of Lucy's attic, how is she related to the other vision that haunts Lucy, the nun of the garret? The figure of the hag-raven goddess endures in Christianity, or so Ross argues, in the image of the benign saint, and the Celtic word *cailleach*, meaning "hag," also means "nun." It is significant, then, that decked out in brilliantly colored clothes and rings, the hunchback comes downstairs from the top of the house to emerge *through the portrait of a dead nun*, the lost Justine Marie, Paul's buried love. Lucy is explicit about the picture, which depicts a madonna-like figure in nun's dress with a pale, young face expressing the dejection of grief, ill health, and acquiescent habits. We have already noted the ways in which Bertha Mason Rochester's aggression is a product of Jane Eyre's submission, and the reasons why Shirley Keeldar's masculine power is a result of Caroline Helstone's feminine immobility. In *Villette*, Madame Walraven's malevolence is likewise the other side of Justine Marie's suicidal passivity. As if dramatizing the truth at the center of Dickinson's poetry—"Ourself behind ourself, concealed—/Should startle most—" (J. 670)—Brontë reveals that the witch *is* the nun. Miss Marchmont's early judgment has, we see, been validated: in a patriarchal society those women who escape becoming either witch or nun must be, like Lucy, haunted by both. For Lucy's ambivalence about love and about men is now fully illuminated: she seeks emotional and erotic involvement as the only available form of self-actualization in her world, yet she fears such involvement will lead either to submission or to destruction, suicide or homicide.

As an androgynous "barbarian queen" (chap. 34) possessing demonic powers associated with Eastern enchantment, Madame Walravens resembles Vashti, for she too is an artist, the creator of crafty plots which result in the death of her characters. Her malevolent plotting, however, only solidifies the connection between witchcraft and female artistry, since the source of the witch's power is her image magic, her *buried representations* that cause weakness, disease, and finally death for the represented victim.[30] With all her egotism and energy, Madame Walravens seems to be a black parody of the artist, perhaps of the author herself, because her three-foot height recalls Brontë's own small stature (four feet, nine inches). At the same time, with her silver beard and masculine voice, she is certainly a sort of male manqué, and having attained power by becoming an essential part of patriarchal culture, she uses her arts to further enslave women. In Madame Walravens, then, it is likely that we see Brontë's anxiety about the effect of her creativity on herself and on others. Yet Madame Walravens is not, of course, actually an artist. Her arts are, in fact, just as repressive and manipulative as Madame Beck's magical surveillance was. And although we saw earlier that Madame Beck was the embodiment of Lucy's attempts at repression, now it becomes clear that, as a character in her own right, Madame Beck has "no taste for a monastic life" (chap. 38). Both Madame Beck and Madame Walravens evade the tyranny of Lucy's internal dialectic, but only by becoming like Jael, Heber's wife, custodians of male values, agents of patriarchal culture who enforce the subjugation of others.

In any case, however, some of Lucy's most crucial categories seem to be breaking down at this point, for she is coming to terms finally with a world more complex than her paranoia ever before allowed her to perceive. Even as she rejects Madame Walravens's image magic, then, she realizes that it cannot be equated with the necromantic magic of the woman who rejects patriarchy, seeking power not through the control of others but through her own self-liberation. Power itself does seem to be dangerous, if not fatal, for women: unsupplied with any socially acceptable channel, the independent and creative woman is dubbed crafty, a witch. If she becomes an artist, she faces the possibility of self-destruction; if she does not, she destroys others. But while Vashti embodies the pain of female artistry, Madame Walravens defines the terrible consequences of not becoming an artist, of being contained in a crippling "defeminized" role. The female artist, Brontë implies, must seek to revivify herself. As sibyl, as shaman, as sorceress, she must avoid not only the silence of the nun, but the curse of the witch.

* * *

Lucy, who has already employed image magic (in the burial of Dr. John's letters), knows its powers are feeble compared with the fearsome but liberating force of the necromantic imagination (which dreams of their resurrection as golden hairs). Jane Eyre had experimented with these two very different arts in her dreamlike drawings (where we saw her unconscious impulses emerging prophetically) and in her portraits (where she didactically portrays beautiful Blanche Ingram in contrast to her own puny self to prove she has no chance with Rochester). More anxious than Jane about creativity, Lucy practices only the severely limited arts of sewing, tracing elaborate line engravings, and writing satiric sketches. Yet, by the time she describes the climactic park scenes, Lucy is an accomplished author. What has happened? To begin with, in the course of the novel she has learned to speak with her own voice, to emerge from the shadows: she defends her creed successfully against the persuasions of Père Silas and M. Paul; she speaks out for the lovers to Polly's father, and she stands up against Madame Beck's interference. All these advances are followed by moments of eclipse when she withdraws, but the sum progress is toward self-articulation, and self-dramatization.

In the process of writing her story, moreover, Lucy has become less evasive. Her narrative increasingly defines her as the center of her own concerns, the heroine of her own history. Her spirited capsule summaries of Polly's and Ginevra's romantic escapades prove that she sees the limits, even the comic aspects, of romantic love, and that another love, painful and constant and intellectual, is now more interesting to her. In fact, Lucy's plots have led not to burial but to exorcism, for she is in the process of becoming the author not only of her own life story but of her own life. It is for this reason that the subject of the ending of *Villette* is the problematic nature of the imagination. Having delineated the horrors of restraint and repression, Brontë turns to the possibility of a life consecrated to imagination, in part to come to terms with her own commitment to the creation of fictions that will no longer enslave women.

Bringing together all the characters and images in a grand finale, the park scenes are fittingly begun by the failure of Madame Beck's attempts to control Lucy. The administered sleeping potion does not drug but awakens her; escaping from the school that is now openly designated a den, a convent, and a dungeon, Lucy seems to have been roused by the necromantic imagination to sleepwalk through a dreamt, magical masque depicting her own quest for selfhood. Searching for the circular mirror, the stone basin of water in the moonlit, midnight summer park, Lucy discovers an enchanted place illuminated by the symbols of the imagination—a flaming arch of stars, colored meteors, Egyptian architecture. Under a spell, in a magical, hallucinogenic world of apparitions and ghosts, she notes that "on this whole scene was impressed a dream-like character: every shape was wavering, every movement floating, every voice echo-like—half-mocking, half-uncertain" (chap. 38). And the fact that this is a celebration commemorating a struggle for liberty does not destroy the marvel of such sights, because it so clearly reflects her own newly experienced freedom from constraint.[31] The allusions to art, the Eastern settings, the music, and the sense of magic remind us that Lucy's struggle is both psychological and aesthetic. So she refers to the park as a woody theater, filled with actors engaged in discoveries that will lead to a climax (chap. 38) and a denouement (chap. 39).

In fact, the sequence of events in this dreamy midsummer *Walpurgisnacht* furnishes a microcosm of the novel, as Lucy's imagination summons up before her the spirits that have haunted her past and present life. First she sees the Brettons and commemorates her feeling for Graham in typically spatial terms, describing the tent of Peri Banou she keeps for him: folded in the hollow of her hand, it would expand into a tabernacle if released. Admitting for the first time her love for Dr. John, she nevertheless avoids making herself known, moving on to watch the "papist junta" composed of Père Silas, Madame Beck, and Madame Walravens. As they wait for the arrival of Justine Marie, Lucy conjures up a vision of the dead nun. But she sees, instead, M. Paul arriving with his young ward, the niece named for the departed saint. Although she is jealous, Lucy feels that M. Paul's nun has now finally been buried, and at this point of great suffering, she begins to praise the goddess of truth. As she has repeatedly, Lucy is advocating repression, although it requires her to reenact the conflict between Jael and Sisera, the pain of self-crucifixion. When "the iron [has] entered well [her] soul," she finally believes she has been "renovated."

Significantly, on her return to the school Lucy finds what seems to be the nun of the garret sleeping in her bed. Now, however, she can at last defy the specter, for the park scene appears to have liberated her, enabling her to destroy this symbol of her chastity and confinement. Why does the appearance of Paul's nun lead to the surfacing of Lucy's? As always, Brontë uses the plot to suggest an answer. Following her imagination on the night of the park festival, Lucy had escaped the convent and, in doing so, she had left the door ajar, thus effecting the escape of Ginevra and de Hamal—the dandy who we now learn has been using the nun's disguise to court the coquette. We have already seen how Ginevra and de Hamal represent the self-gratifying, sensual, romantic side of Lucy. Posturing before mirrors, the fop and the coquette are vacuous but for the roles they play. Existing only in the "outside" world, they have no more sense of self than the nun whose life is completely "internal." Thus, for Lucy to liberate herself from Ginevra and de Hamal means that she can simultaneously rid herself of the self-denying nun. In fact, these mutually dependent spirits have been cast out of her house because, in the park, unable to withdraw into voyeurism, she experienced jealousy. Hurt without being destroyed, she has at least temporarily liberated herself from the dialectic of her internal schism. And to indicate once again how that split is a male fiction, Brontë shows us how the apparently female image of the nun masks the romantic male plots of de Hamal.

What is most ironic about this entire sequence, however, is that Lucy is wrong: Paul is committed to her, not to the memory of the buried Justine Marie, or to his ward. But, because she is wrong, she is saved. Imagination has led her astray throughout the park scene—conjuring up an image of a calm and shadowy park and then leading her to believe that she can exist invisibly in the illuminated festival, causing her to picture Madame Beck in her bed and M. Paul on shipboard, creating the romantic story of Paul and his rich, beautiful ward. It is with relieved self-mockery that Lucy laughs at her own panegyric to the so-called goddess of truth, whose message is really only an imaginative projection of her own worst fears. Ultimately, indeed, the entire distinction between imagination and reason breaks down in the park scenes because Lucy realizes that what she has called "Reason" is really repressive witchcraft or image magic that would transform her into a nun. Although Lucy leaves the park thinking that the calm, white, stainless moon triumphs—a witness of "truth all regnant" (chap. 39)—the next day she cannot accept the truth. And though she views it as a weakness, this very inability to acquiesce in silence is a sign of her freedom from the old internal struggle, for Lucy has emerged from the park a more integrated person, able to express herself in the most threatening circumstances. Now she can even defy Madame Beck to catch at a last chance to speak with Paul, detaining him with her cry: "My heart will break!" (chap. 41).

And, albeit with terrible self-consciousness, Lucy can now ask Paul whether her appearance displeases him. This question climaxes a series of scenes before the mirror, each of which defines Lucy's sense of herself. When, at the beginning of the book, Ginevra shows Lucy an image of herself with no attractive accomplishments, no beauty, no chance of love, the girl accepts the reflection with satiric calm, commending Ginevra's honesty. Midway through the novel, however, at the concert, she experiences a "jar of discord, a pang of regret" (chap. 20) at the contrast between herself in a pink dress and the handsome Brettons. Finally, when she thinks she has lost the last opportunity of seeing Paul, she feelingly perceives herself alone— sodden, white, with swollen and glassy eyes (chap. 38). Instead of seeing the mirror-image as the object of another person's observations, Lucy looks at herself by herself. Increasingly able to identify herself with her body, she is freed from the contradictory and stultifying definitions of her provided by all those who think they know her, and she begins to understand how Dr. John, Mr. Home, Ginevra, and even Polly see her in a biased way. At last, Brontë suggests, Lucy has learned that imaginative "projection" and reasoned "apprehension" of the "truth" are inseparable. The mirror does not reflect reality; it creates it by interpreting it. But the act of interpretation can avoid tyranny when it remains just that—a perceptual act. After all, "wherever an accumulation of small defences is found . . . there, be sure, it is needed" (chap. 27).

It is this mature recognition of the necessity and inadequacy of self-definition—this understanding of the need for fictions that assert their own limits by proclaiming their personal usefulness—that wins for Lucy finally a room of her own, indeed, a house of her own. The school in the Faubourg Clotilde is a fitting conclusion to her struggle and to the struggles of all of Brontë's heroines for a comfortable space. The small house has large, vine-covered windows. The salon is tiny, but pretty, with delicate walls tinged like a blush and a brilliant carpet covering the highly waxed floor. The small furniture, the plants, the diminutive kitchenware please Lucy. Not by any means a dwelling too wide for walls or too high for dome, her tidy house represents on the one hand the lowering of her sights and on the other her willingness to begin making her own way, even if on a small scale.

Both a home and a school, the house represents Lucy's independence: upstairs are two sleeping-rooms and a schoolroom—no attic mentioned. Here, on the balcony, overlooking the gardens of the faubourg, near a water-jet rising from a nearby well, Paul and Lucy commemorate their love in a simple meal that consists of chocolate, rolls, and fresh red fruit. Although he is her king, her provider only rents the house himself and she will quickly have to earn her keep: Lucy has escaped both the ancestral mansion and the convent. And so, under the moonlight that is now an emblem of her imaginative power to define her own truths, she is more fortunate than Shirley because she actually experiences the days of "our great Sire and Mother"; she can "taste that grand morning's dew—bathe in its sunrise" (chap. 41).

Unlike Caroline Helstone, moreover, Lucy is given real food, for she is to be sustained by Paul, even in his absence: "he would give neither a stone, nor an excuse—neither a scorpion, nor a disappointment; his letters were real food that nourished, living water that refreshed" (chap. 42). Nevertheless, despite her hope that women can obtain a full, integrated sense of themselves *and* economic independence *and* male affection, Brontë also recognizes that such a wish must not be presented falsely as an accomplished fact. The ambiguous ending of *Villette* reflects Lucy's ambivalence, her love for Paul and her recognition that it is only in his absence that she can exert herself fully to exercise her own powers. It also reflects Brontë's determination to avoid the tyrannical fictions that have traditionally victimized women. Once more, she deflates male romanticism. Although her lover sails off on the *Paul et Virginie*, although her novel—like Bernadin de Saint Pierre's—ends in shipwreck, Brontë insists again that it is the confined woman, Lucy, who waits at home for the adventuring male, but notes that the end of love must not be equated with the end of life. The last chapter of *Villette* begins by reminding us that "Fear sometimes imagines a vain thing" (chap. 42). It ends with Lucy's refusal to end conclusively: "Leave sunny imaginations hope" (chap. 42). Brontë gives us an open-ended, elusive fiction, refraining from any definitive message except to remind us of the continued need for sustaining stories of survival.

The very erratic way Lucy tells the story of becoming the author of her own life illustrates how Brontë produces not a literary object but a literature of consciousness. Just as Brontë has become Lucy Snowe for the writing of *Villette*, just as Lucy has become all her characters, we submit to the spell of the novel, to the sepulchral voice relating truths of the dead revivified by the necromancy of the imagination. Brontë rejects not only the confining images conferred on women by patriarchal art, but the implicitly coercive nature of that art. *Villette* is not meticulously crafted. The very excess of its style, as well as the ambiguous relationship between its author and its heroine, declare Brontë's commitment to the personal processes of writing and reading. In place of the ecstatic or philosophic egotistical sublime, she offers us something closer to the qualified experience of what Keats called "negative capability." Making her fiction a parodic, confessional utterance that can only be understood through the temporal sequences of its plot, Brontë criticizes the artists she considers in *Villette*—Rubens, Schiller, Bernadin de Saint Pierre, Wordsworth, Arnold, and others.

It is ironic that her protest could not save her from being the subject of one of Arnold's poetic complaints on the early death of poets. In "Haworth Churchyard" Arnold recognizes how Brontë's art is lit by intentionality when he describes how she told "With a Master's accent her feign'd History of passionate life." But his insistence on desexing her art—here, by describing her "Master's accent," later by referring to her with a masculine pronoun[32]—

shows him to be the first of a long line of readers who could not or would not submit to a reading process and a realization so totally at odds with his own life, his own art and criticism.

It is the act of receptivity that Brontë uses to subvert patriarchal art. Recently some feminists have been disturbed that Brontë did not reject the passivity of her heroines.[33] As we have seen, her books do elaborate on the evils of equating masculinity with power and femininity with submission. But Brontë knew that the habit of submission had bequeathed a vital insight to women—a sympathetic imagination that could help them, in their revolt, from becoming like their masters. Having been obliged to experience themselves as objects, women understand both their need and their capacity for awakening from a living death; they know it is necromancy, not image magic—a resurrecting confessional art, not a crucifying confessional penance—which can do this without entangling yet another Other in what they have escaped. Conscious of the politics of poetics, Brontë is, in some ways, a phenomenologist—attacking the discrepancy between reason and imagination, insisting on the subjectivity of the objective work of art, choosing as the subject of her fiction the victims of objectification, inviting her readers to experience with her the interiority of the Other. For all these reasons she is a powerful precursor for all the women who have been strengthened by the haunted and haunting honesty of her art.

NOTES

Epigraphs: The Prisoner of Chillon, lines 389-91; letter to W.S. Williams, 26 July 1849; Poems, J. 670; "the Prisoner," *Here Comes and Other Poems* (New York: Signet, 1975), p. 229

1. Letter to W.S. Williams, 6 November. 1852, in The Brontes: Their Lives, Friendship and Correspondence, ed. T.J. Wise and J. Alexander Symington (Oxford: Blackwell, 1932), 4:18.

2. Ibid.

3. "Frances," in *Poems of Charlotte and Branwell Bronte*, ed. T. J. Wise and J. Alexander Symington (Oxford: Shakespeare Head, 1934), pp. 20-28

4. Matthew Arnold, "The Buried Life," lines 73 and 87.

5. This is precisely the irony that Anthony Hecht exploits in his parody "the Dover Bitch."

6. William Wordsworth, "A Slumber Did My Spirit Seal," line 3. The other Wordsworth poems to which we allude in the text are: "She Dwealt Among the Untrodden Ways," "I traveled Among Unknown Men," "Strange Fits of Passion Have I Known," "Three Years She Grew in Sun and Shower," and "Lucy Gray."

7. Charlotte Bronte, *Villete* (New York: Harper Colophon, 19720, chap. 26. All subsequent references will be to this edition.

8. While most critics refer to a struggle between reason and imagination that remains abstract and oddly devoid of psychological meaning, Margot Peters persuasively place this antithesis is the larger debate over asserting one's identity in a hostile world. See *Charlotte Bronte: Style in the Novel* (Madison; University of Wisconsin Press, 1973), pp. 119-21. Also Andrew D. Hook, "Charlott Bronte, the Imagination, and *Villete*," in The Brontes: A Collection of Critical Essays, ed. Ian Gregor, pp. 137-56

9. In her introduction to Harper Colophon *Villete,* Q. D. Leavis argues that "little Polly is an externalization of [Lucy's] inner self," p. xxvi.

10. See, for example, Robert Martin, *The Accents of Persuasion,* (New York: Norton, 1966), P 153.

11. In her review of *Villette* in the *Daily News,* 3 February 1853, Harriet Martineau. Complains that "All of the female character, in all their thoughts and lives, are full of one thing, or are regarded by the reader in the light of that one thought –love." This review is reprinted in The Brontes: The Critical Heritage, ed. Miriam Allcott (London and Boston: Routledge & Keegan Paul, 1974), pp. 171-74.

12. Richard Lovelace, "to *Althea,* from prison," lines 25-26.

13. Even as brilliant a critic as Q. D. Leavis considers the nun only a "bogus supernatural theme," used by Bronte to maintain suspense and to get the book published. See her introducition to the Harper Colophon *Villete* p. xxiii.   Also, Nina Auerbach, "Charlotte Bronte: The Two Countries," *University of Toronto Quarterly* 42 (Summer 1973) : 339, argues in an otherwise insightful essay that the plot is unrelated to Lucy's struggle for identity. Of course there have been several important critical responses to these attacks; probably the most important is still Robert B. Heilman's "Charlotte Bronte's 'New' Gothic," in *From Jane Austen to Joseph Conrad,* ed. Robert C. Rathburn and Martin Steinmann, Jr. (Minneapolis: University of Minnesota Press, 1958), pp. 188-32

14. George Eliot, Westminster review 65 (January, 1856): 290-312

15. Barbara Charlesworth Gelpi and Albert Gelpi, eds., "When We Dead Awaken," Adrienne Rich's poetry (New York: Norton, 1975), p. 59

16. Max Byrd, "The Madhouse, The Whorehouse and the Convent," *Partisan Review* (Summer 1977), discusses depictions of incest within convents by "Monk" Lewis, E.T.A. Hoffman, and Diderot.

17. Christina Rosetti, " Cobwebs," in Lona Mask Packer, *Christina Rosetti*(Berkeley and Los Angeles: University of California Press, 1963), p.99

18. Nina Auerbach, *Communities of Women: An Idea in Fiction* (Cambridge, Mass.: Harvard University Press, 1978), p. 109.

19. E.M. Forster, Aspects of the Novel (New York: Harcourt, Brace, 1964), pp. 92-93

20. Kate Millet, Sexual Politics (New York: Avon, 1971), p. 198

21. Martin, *Accents of Persuasion*, pp. 166-60; See Andrew D Hook, "Charlotte Bronte, the Imagination and *Villette* " for an excellent discussion of Lucy's incoherence in describing Vashti, p. 151. Vashti's story appears in the Book of Esther, 1:1 to 2:18

22. Frances Harper, "Vashti," in Early Black American Poets, ed. William Robinson (Iowa: Wm. C. Brown Co. 1969), pp. 34-36

23. In *Charolotte Bronte*, p.481, Winifred Gerin explains that Rachel was most famous for her passionate role in *Phedre,* but that Charolotte Bronte saw her act the "milder" roles of Camille in Corneille's *Les Trois Horaces* and Adrienne in *Adrienne Lecouvreur.*

24. Sylvia Plath, "lady Lazarus, " *Ariel,* pp. 6-9

25. Charles Burkhart, *Charolotte Bronte; A Psychosexual Study of Her Novels* (London: Victor Gollancz Ltd., 1973), pp. 113-17; Heilman, "Bronte's 'New' Gothic"; E.D.H. Johnson, "'Daring the Dread Glance': Charlotte Bronte's treatment of the Supernatural in *Villette,* " *Nineteenth-Century Fiction 20* (March 1966): 325-36

26. Sylvia Plath, "Small Hours," *Crossing the Water* (New York: Harper & Row, 1971), P 28.

27. The most recent feminist exploration of the nun as a symbol of female self-abnegation appears in Mona Isabel Berrano, Maria Teresa Horta and Maria Velho da Costa, The Three Marias, trans. Helen R. Lane (New York: Bantam, 1975).

28. Bell Gale Chevigny*, The Woman and the Myth: Margaret Fuller's Life and Writing* (Old Westbury, N.Y.: The Feminist Press, 1976,) p.440

29. Anne Ross, "The Divine Hag of the Pagan Celts," in The Witch Figure, ed. Venetia Newall (London: Routledge & Kegan Paul, 1973), p.162

30. George Lyman Kittredge, *Witchcraft in Old and New England* (New York: Russell and Russell, 1929), pp. 73-103

31. Earl A Knies, *The Art of Charolotte Bronte* (Athens, Ohio: Ohio University Press, 1969), p. 194.

32. Matthew Arnold's "Haworth Churchyard" originally appeared in *Fraser's Magazine,* May 1855, and is reprinted in *The Brontes,* ed. Allot, pp. 306-10.

33. Patricia Beer, "*Reader, I Married Him,*" pp 84-126, and Patricia Meyer Spacks, The Female Imagination, pp. 70-72

Chronology

1812   Reverend Patrick Brontë marries and Maria Branwell.

1813   Maria Brontë born at Hartshead.

1815   Elizabeth Brontë born at Hartshead.

1816   Charlotte Brontë born at Thornton on April 21.

1817   Patrick Branwell Brontë, the only son, born at Thornton in June.

1818   Emily Jane Brontë born at Thornton on July 30.

1820   Anne Brontë born on January 17 at Thornton; Reverend Patrick appointed to incumbency of Haworth, family moves to Haworth near Bradford, Yorkshire.

1821   Mrs. Brontë dies of cancer in September.

1823   Aunt Elizabeth Branwell comes to Haworth.

1824   Maria and Elizabeth attend the Clergy Daughters' School at Cowan Bridge Clergy Daughters' School; Charlotte and Emily arrive later.

1825   Maria and Elizabeth contract tuberculosis and leave Cowan Bridge. Maria dies on May 6; Elizabeth dies June 15. Charlotte and Emily are withdrawn from the school and continue their education at home.

1826	Inspired by a box of wooden soldiers, the four remaining Brontë children begin writing about imaginary worlds. Charlotte and Branwell begin the "Angrian" stories; Emily and Anne work on the "Gondal" saga.
1831	Charlotte enters Miss Wooler's school at Roe Head where she meets lifelong friends Ellen Nussey and Mary Taylor.
1832	Charlotte leaves Roe Head to attend to her sisters' educations.
1835	Charlotte returns to Roe Head as a governess; Emily enrolls at Roe Head, but returns home later home sick and in poor health; Branwell travels to London.
1836	Anne enrolls at Roe Head, where she remains until 1837; Branwell opens a portrait studio in Bradford.
1837	Emily becomes a governess at Miss Patchett's school, near Halifax.
1838	Charlotte resigns her position at Roe Head and returns home.
1839	Anne becomes governess for Mrs. Ingham at Blake Hall, Mirfield; Charlotte becomes governess for Mrs. Sidgwick at Stonegap Hall, near Skipton.
1840	Branwell becomes a tutor, then a railway clerk; Anne takes a position as governess for the Robinson family.
1842	Charlotte and Emily enroll at the Pensionnat Héger in Brussels; Aunt Branwell dies and they return home; Branwell dismissed as railway clerk.
1843	Charlotte returns to Brussels as a teacher; Branwell joins Anne as tutor at Thorp Green.
1844	Charlotte returns home; the sisters attempt to start a school at Haworth.
1845	Rev. A. B. Nicholls arrives at Haworth; Branwell is dismissed from Thorp Green; Anne also leaves.
1846	Publication of *Poems of Currer, Ellis, and Acton Bell*, pseudonyms for Charlotte, Emily, and Anne.
1847	Publication of *Jane Eyre* by Charlotte, *Wuthering Heights* by Emily, and *Agnes Grey* by Anne.

1848   Publication of *The Tenant of Wildfell Hall* by Anne; Branwell dies of tuberculosis, September 24; Emily dies of the same, December 19.

1849   Anne dies of tuberculosis, May 28; publication of *Shirley* by Charlotte.

1850   Charlotte meets Elizabeth Gaskell.

1853   Publication of *Villette* by Charlotte.

1854   Charlotte marries Rev. A. B. Nicholls, June 29.

1855   Charlotte dies of toxemia of pregnancy, March 31.

1857   *Life of Charlotte Brontë* by Mrs. Gaskell is published; *The Professor*, by Charlotte, is published posthumously.

1860   "Emma" a fragment of a story by Charlotte is published

1861   Patrick Brontë dies, June 7.

Works by the Brontë Sisters

ANNE BRONTË

The Poems of Currer, Ellis, and Acton Bell 1846.
Agnes Grey 1847.
The Tenant of Wildfell Hall 1848.

CHARLOTTE BRONTË

The Poems of Currer, Ellis, and Acton Bell 1846.
Jane Eyre 1847.
Shirley 1849.
Villette 1853.
The Professor 1857.

EMILY BRONTË

The Poems of Currer, Ellis, and Acton Bell 1846.
Wuthering Heights 1847

Works about the Brontë Sisters

Allot, Miriam, ed. *The Brontës: The Critical Heritage*. London: Routledge and Kegan Paul, 1974.

Armstrong, Nancy. *Desire and Domestic Fiction*. New York: Oxford University Press, 1987.

Auerbach, Nina. *Woman and the Demon: The Life of a Victorian Myth*. Cambridge, Mass.: Harvard University Press, 1982.

Barker, Juliet. *The Brontës*. New York: St. Martin's Press, 1994.

Bentley, Phyllis. *The Brontës and Their World*. New York: Viking, 1969.

Boehmer, Elleke. *Colonial and Postcolonial Literature*. New York: Oxford University Press, 1995.

Blom, Margaret Howard. *Charlotte Brontë*. Boston: Twayne Publishing, 1977.

Clarke, Michael M. "Brontë's *Jane Eyre* and the Grimms' Cinderella" *Studies in English Literature, 1500–1900* 40 (2000): 695–710.

Daleski, H.M. *The Divided Heroine*. New York: Holmes and Meier Publishers, 1984.

Edwards, Mike. *Charlotte Brontë: The Novels*. New York: Oxford University Press, 1990.

Ewbank, Inga-Stina. *Their Proper Sphere: A Study of the Brontë Sisters as Early Victorian Female Novelists*. Cambridge, Mass.: Harvard University Press, 1966.

Forsyth, Beverly. "The Two Faces of Lucy Snowe: A Study in Deviant Behavior" *Studies in the Novel* 29 (1997): 17–25.

Frawley, Maria. H. *Anne Brontë*. New York: Twayne Publishers, 1996.

Gardiner, Juliet. *The Brontës at Haworth: The World Within*. New York: Clarkson Potter Publishers, 1992.

Gaskell, Elizabeth. *The Life of Charlotte Brontë*. Harmondsworth, England: Penguin, 1975.

Guzetti, Paula. *A Family Called Brontë*. New York: Dillon Press, 1994.

Horsman, Alan. *The Victorian Novel*. New York: Oxford University Press, 1990.

Knapp, Bettina L. *The Brontës: Branwell, Anne, Emily, Charlotte*. New York: Continuum, 1991.

Learner, Laurence. "Bertha and the Critics." *Nineteenth Century Literature*. 44, (1989):273–300.

Peters, Margot. *Unquiet Soul: A Biography of Charlotte Brontë*. New York: Atheneum, 1986.

Pool, Daniel. *Dickens' Fur Coat and Charlotte's Unanswered Letters, The Rows and Romances of England's Great Victorian Novelists*. New York: HarperPerennial Library, 1998.

Ross, Stewart. *Charlotte Brontë and Jane Eyre*. New York: Viking, 1997.

Schlossberg, Herbert. *The Silent Revolution and the Making of Victorian England*. Cincinnati: Ohio State University Press, 2000.

Scott, P.J.M. *Anne Brontë: A New Critical Assessment*. New York: Barnes and Noble, 1983.

Senf, Carol. "Emily Brontë's Version of Feminist History: *Wuthering Heights*." *Essays in Literature* 12 (1985): 201–214.

Showalter, Elaine. *A Literature of Their Own: British Women Novelists from Brontë to Lessing*. Princeton: Princeton University Press, 1977.

Smith, Anne, ed. *The Art of Anne Brontë*. London: Vision Press, 1976.

Swisher, Clarice. *Turning Points in World History: Victorian England*. San Diego, Calif.: Greenhaven Press, 2000.

Warhol, Robyn R. "Double Gender, Double Genre in *Jane Eyre* and *Villette*." *Studies in English Literature, 1500–1900* 36 (1996): 857–875.

Yaeger, Patricia. "Violence in the Sitting Room: *Wuthering Heights* and the Woman's Novel." *Genre* 21 (1988): 203–229.

WEBSITES

The Brontë Sisters Web (accessed 3/28/02):
   www.lang.nagoya-u.ac.jp/~matsuoka/Bronte.html
Brontë Country (accessed 3/28/02)
   www.bronte-country.com/brontes.html
The Gaskell Web (accessed 3/28/02):
   www.lang.nagoya-u.ac.jp/~matsuoka/Gaskell.html
The Victorian Web (accessed 3/28/02):
   http://www.victorianweb.org
Brontë Parsonage Museum (accessed 3/28/02):
   www.bronte.org.uk/

Contributors

HAROLD BLOOM is Sterling Professor of the Humanities at Yale University and Henry W. and Albert A. Berg Professor of English at the New York University Graduate School. He is the author of over 20 books, including *Shelly's Mythmaking* (1959), *The Visionary Company* (1961), *Blake's Apocalypse* (1963), *Yeats* (1970), *A Map of Misreading* (1975), *Kabbalah and Criticism* (1975), *Agon: Toward a Theory of Revisionism* (1982), *The American Religion* (1992), *The Western Canon* (1994), and *Omens of Millennium: The Gnosis of Angels, Dreams, and Resurrection* (1996). *The Anxiety of Influence* (1973) sets forth Professor Bloom's provocative theory of the literary relationships between the great writers and their predecessors. His most recent books include *Shakespeare: The Invention of the Human*, a 1998 National Book Award finalist, and *How to Read and Why*, which was published in 2000. In 1999, Professor Bloom received the prestigious American Academy of Arts and Letters Gold Medal for Criticism.

NORMA JEAN LUTZ is a freelance writer who lives in Tulsa, Oklahoma. She is the author of more than 250 short stories and articles as well as over 50 books of fiction and nonfiction.

KAREN WEYANT is a Developmental English and Writing Instructor at Jamestown Community College, Jamestown, NY, where she teaches a variety of writing and literature classes.

T. E. APTER'S other works of literature criticism include *Thomas Mann, the Devil's Advocate*, and *Virginia Woolf: A Study of Her Novels*.

In addition to having written The Brontë Novels, **W. A. CRAIK** has made significant contributions to the scholarship on Jane Austen.

SANDRA GILBERT and **SUSAN GUBAR** have collaborated on a number of projects, and are among the most noted feminist critics. Together they are the authors of *Shakespeare's Sisters: Feminist Essays on Women Poets, The Madwoman in the Attic, and No Man's Land: The Place of the Woman Writer in the Twentieth Century*. They also co-edited *The Norton Anthology of Literature by Women*.

Index

160 · INDEX

British colonization theme in,
61–2
Byronic hero in, 55–6
Catherine and Heathcliffe grieving
eachother in, 70–1
Catherine and Heathcliffe's love
for eachother in, 71–2
Catherine's death in, 75–6
Cathy Linton character in, 78–80
emotional intensity in, 74–5
emotional outbursts in, 72–4
gothic elements in, 54
Heathcliffe's death in, 77–8
Heathcliffe's lack of envying

Catherine in, 69–70
Heathcliffe's misanthropy in, 67
influence of, 50
Law School and, 29
love and death theme in, 68–9
publication of, 1
reviews of, 43
romantic longing in, 76–7
Romantic tradition in, 65–7
trappings of marriage theme in, 58
as without moral design, 67–8

Young Men's Magazine, 20